In this fine book, Barbara Duguid combines her love of church history, her enthusiasm for John Newton, her insights honed as a pastor's wife, and above all her love for Christ and his church. Here the reader will find sharp insights into the psychology of sin and sound practical advice on how the Bible speaks to the mundane rebellions of everyday human existence, The heart is indeed restless above all things; Barbara Duguid ably directs us to where we can find rest: in Christ alone.

—**Carl R. Trueman,** Paul Woolley Professor of Church History, Westminster Theological Seminary, Philadelphia; Pastor, Cornerstone Presbyterian Church (OPC), Ambler, Pennsylvania

Consider this: "What if growing in grace is more about humility, dependence, and exalting Christ than it is about defeating sin?" No, this is not heresy; this is deft and loving pastoral care. If you are earnest in your desire to follow Jesus but wondering why you still feel like such a sinner, this is the perfect book for you.

—**Edward T. Welch,** Faculty Member, Christian Counseling and Education Foundation

John Newton was such a good pastor because he understood so well sin, suffering, and the amazing grace of Jesus Christ, and it helps to hear from those who are familiar with his work, summarizing it in light of their own faith journey. Barb Duguid has done today's church a great service by sharing with us her fine overview of Newton's understanding of the Christian soul. Feast, be encouraged, and be built up.

—**Eric Johnson,** Lawrence and Charlotte Hoover Professor of Pastoral Care, The Southern Baptist Theological Seminary, Louisville, Kentucky; Society for Christian Psychology

Stay away from this book! Barb Duguid makes idolatry too nauseating, grace too promiscuous, the Trinity too omnipotent, Christian experience too diverse, sanctification too scary, and sovereignty too comforting.

—**Dale Ralph Davis,** Teaching Pastor, Woodland Presbyterian Church, Hattiesburg, Mississippi

The way many Christians think about sanctification is, well, not very sanctified. In fact it's downright narcissistic. We think way too much about how we're doing, if we're growing, whether we're doing it right or not. We spend too much time brooding over our failures and reflecting on our successes. What I've discovered is that the more I focus on my need to get better, the worse I actually get. I become self-absorbed, which is the exact opposite of how the Bible describes what it means to be sanctified. This is why I was shouting, "Yes, yes!" again and again as I read Barbara's excellent book.

Over and over again Barbara reminds us that spiritual growth is not arriving at some point where we need Jesus less and less because we're getting better and better; it's realizing how utterly dependent we are on Christ's cross and mercy.

—**Tullian Tchividjian,** Pastor, Coral Ridge Presbyterian Church, Fort Lauderdale; Author, *Jesus + Nothing = Everything*

Barbara is qualified to bring you a message of extravagant grace because she has drunk deeply of it herself. She knows that, along with John Newton, she is a great sinner who has a great Savior and it is this message of God's mercy to undeserving sinners that will encourage you to live in the light of the sweetest news ever heard: "He died for a wretch like me!"

—**Elyse Fitzpatrick,** Author, *Idols of the Heart*; Conference Speaker

Weaving together the delightful insights of John Newton with her own experience and that of many people she's counseled over the years, Barb tells the story of God's unrelenting compassion toward sinners like us with profound wisdom. How amazing is grace? Like Newton, Barb has learned well the answer to that question from the greatest storyteller of all.

—**Michael S. Horton,** J. Gresham Machen Professor of Systematic Theology and Apologetics, Westminster Seminary California

If only there were some secret—a strategy, an answer, a truth, a fix—to end all the awkward struggle in life! There is a way to live, however, that teaches us to struggle well through the wrongs inside us and around us. Barb Duguid struggles well. She has learned well from another lifelong struggler, John Newton. Both of them learned well from the Man of sorrows and grace.

—**David Powlison,** Faculty Member, Christian Counseling and Education Foundation

extravagant grace

extravagant grace

GOD'S GLORY DISPLAYED
IN OUR WEAKNESS

Barbara R. Duguid

P U B L I S H I N G
P.O. BOX 817 • PHILLIPSBURG • NEW JERSEY 08865-0817

ISBN: 978-1-59638-449-1 (pbk)
ISBN: 978-1-59638-941-0 (ePub)
ISBN: 978-1-59638-942-7 (Mobi)

Printed in the United States of America

Library of Congress Control Number: 2013943699

For Wayne,
my dearly beloved son,
who loves Newton and needs Jesus almost as much as I do,
and who persuaded me to write this book.

Now to him who is able to keep you from stumbling and to present you blameless before the presence of his glory with great joy, to the only God, our Savior, through Jesus Christ our Lord, be glory, majesty, dominion, and authority, before all time and now and forever. Amen. (Jude 24–25)

Contents

Foreword

This book has been a long time in the making. It had its roots in our time in seminary in Philadelphia, when Tim Keller recommended that Barb read *The Letters of John Newton* as a resource to understanding the Christian life. Specifically, her concern was the fact that those areas of her life where she sought to battle sin most energetically were precisely the areas where she seemed to be making least progress. Since then, John Newton's warm, pastoral, and grace-centered understanding of sanctification has had a steadily increasing effect on Barb's thinking (and my own).

Yet this topic has never been an abstract intellectual field of inquiry for Barb. As one of the most honest people I know, she has wrestled through the practical application of these truths in her own battles with indwelling sin, as you will read in these pages. In addition, as she has grown in her own understanding, she has been able to share those insights with others in the counseling room, in small group Bible studies, and on church retreats. Many have been blessed through her ministry with a new understanding of the dynamics of God's grace at work in the midst of our sin.

It is not news to most Christians that the gospel of God's grace is good news and that we also need to grow in our holiness. The challenge is putting these two truths together in a biblical way. Some have perhaps so emphasized God's grace that people lose sight of striving toward the goal of holiness, while others put so much stress on the need for holiness that, for struggling sinners, Christianity seems hardly to be good news anymore. For many, our understanding of how God thinks about us is shaped by the old children's hymn.

> Jesus loves me when I'm good, when I do the things I should.
> Jesus loves me when I'm bad, though it makes him very sad.

As a result, we have come to believe that God's favor rests upon us when we obey, but when we disobey (which for most of us is much of the time), he is deeply disappointed in us. This leads many to wrestle with a pervasive sense of failure and guilt, which results in a lack of the joy and peace that we read so much about in the Bible.

In this book, you will read how God's grace to us in Christ is the best news precisely when our struggle with sin is most intense. God's extravagant and sovereign grace really is greater than all of our sin!

Iain Duguid

Acknowledgments

I am completely dependent upon John Newton for every brilliant thought you will read in this book. Where I have not quoted him directly, I have paraphrased him liberally, and can therefore take no credit whatsoever for either the profound depth of biblical truth or the grace-saturated applications of those doctrines. At times I have taken his thoughts further than he did and applied them to life in ways that he didn't, but I am hopeful he would agree with what I have done and add his amen.

Tim Keller was the first to direct me to the letters of John Newton twenty-eight years ago. I am deeply indebted to him and Kathy for their love and support during our seminary years, and for modeling the gospel in living Technicolor for us during that formative time.

There are many people to thank for their participation in writing this book. My parents, Sam and Pat Befus, first planted the seed of faith in my heart and watered it faithfully. I thank them for their devotion to Christ, for their editorial help, and for being enthusiastic cheerleaders all along the way. My husband, Iain, has been my hero and champion in the writing process. He took my jumbled thoughts, brought order to chaos, and earned my undying admiration and gratitude all along the way.

I want to thank my children, Wayne, Jamie, Sam, Peggy, Hannah, Rob, and Rosie. Watching them grow in grace has been the greatest delight and honor of my lifetime, and when I hear them comfort me with the words of John Newton, my heart giggles with glee and worships the One who has promised to be their God as well as mine. He has surely kept that promise.

I would like to thank Matt Harmon, Ralph Davis, and Eric Johnson for their helpful comments on the manuscript, and Amanda Martin for her editorial help. I am grateful to Bryce Craig and his team at P&R for giving me this opportunity, and to Aaron Gottier, my project manager, for his patience with my jitters.

I am grateful to Louise Schmidtberger and Kim Ware for their great enthusiasm and faithful prayer, especially when I got stuck and thought I would never finish. I am also indebted to all the young women who have studied Newton with me over the years and loved the truths that he teaches. They have sharpened me with their questions and delighted me with their hunger to grow. I especially thank Kat Kuciemba, Michelle Bowser, Larissa Lisk, and Carolyn Wise for drinking deeply at this fountain with me. I also thank Elyse Fitzpatrick for her friendship and encouragement to write, and Kathy Daane, editor of *Anchor Magazine*, for giving me my first opportunity to explore these ideas in print.

I praise God that all the wonderful principles explored in this book are absolutely true and freely given to each beloved child he has joined to his Son, Jesus Christ. Whether we stand or fall, run the race or have only enough faith to keep looking in the right direction, he is faithful to us. He will use all of creation, through his powerful Holy Spirit, for his own glory and the spiritual and eternal good of his children. Praise God that we are not under law but are privileged to thrive under his luxurious and extravagant grace.

Preface

Everywhere I go I meet Christians who are depressed, anxious, and discouraged because they still sin. In fact, the sins that they try the hardest to conquer and triumph over are often the very ones that they cannot defeat. Many of these people attend churches that believe and preach the Bible and love the Word of God passionately. They read their Bibles, desiring to live lives of growing obedience. They pray eagerly, sincerely asking God to change them. Every now and then they attend a retreat or hear a sermon, and with renewed energy and determination, they make a plan to beat this sin once and for all. They pray and fast, they memorize Scripture and attend accountability groups, they write in journals. For a while, it seems to work and things get better. But before long, their old sin creeps back in and once again wins the day. Only now it is even worse than before. Now discouragement wells up like a tsunami of shame as hope of real change is shattered once again.

Many Christians suffer from this relentless cycle of conviction, repentance, efforts to change, and complete defeat. They read about the joyful, victorious Christian life and think that God must be so disappointed in them because it does not describe their experience. Perhaps they conclude that they must not be saved at all.

So why do real Christians still sin so much, even after they have been saved for decades? Why can't we just get our act together and keep getting better? What is God up to in allowing so much disobedience and disgrace to remain in the lives and churches of his beloved people? If sanctification is all about us sinning less and less, then we would have to conclude that the Holy Spirit isn't doing his job very well. Even the apostle Paul called himself the chief of sinners toward the end of his apostolic career (1 Tim. 1:15). Instead of growing out of his sin, it seems that he was seeing more and more of it.

Perhaps our greatest problem is not the reality of our sin, but our unbiblical expectations of what Christian growth should look like. What if growing in grace is more about humility, dependence, and exalting Christ than it is about defeating sin? How would that impact our struggle with sin and our joy in Christ as we continue to live as weak sinners in a fallen world? Surely it would make all the difference in the world!

This book will seek to recover a more biblical theology of sin and sanctification, a theology that was familiar and dear to the wise pastors who framed the Westminster Confession of Faith and to their successors. In particular, we will take a fresh look at the writings of John Newton, the former slave trader turned Anglican minister who wrote the well-known hymn, "Amazing Grace." This eighteenth-century pastor outlined a theology of sinful failure that humbles weak sinners, magnifies the finished work of Jesus Christ, and comforts people who just can't seem to stop sinning by pointing them to Christ in their worst moments of defeat. This is a truth that has been largely lost to a contemporary church overwhelmed by individual triumphalism and the myth of the victorious Christian life. As a result, many Christians live lives of deep discouragement and anguish, hiding their shameful struggles from one another.

It is a radical and almost frightening thought to see that God is actually as much at work in our worst moments of sin and defeat as he is in our best moments of shining obedience. Far from leading us further into sin, this concept draws us into

deeper dependence on the promises and the power of God. If he
who started a good work in us has promised to complete it, then
we are safe. If Scripture shows us a God who is absolutely sovereign over the sins of all people, even those of his own children,
then we may be comforted. If God uses our ongoing sin to show
us the breathtaking beauty of our Savior, we will be captivated.
If our ongoing sin keeps us at the foot of the cross, desperately
in need of a refuge and redeemer, then the party starts here and
now and my daily sin becomes the conduit for outrageous joy
and celebration. So let the festivities begin.

In this book I am demonstrating a progressive work of grace
through stories. The stories are all true, though in some places
names have been changed to protect the guilty! Most of the
stories involve me—not because I am trying to proclaim what
a wonderful person I am; in fact, quite the contrary. They are
about me because mine is the only heart I really know much
about, and my sin is the only sin on which I can speak with some
degree of expertise.

The stories you will read are meant to connect great and
mighty doctrinal truths to the minutes and hours of everyday
life. It is wonderful to study God's truth, but it is far better to
take that truth and dress up in it day after day: to work in it,
play in it, sleep in it, party in it, and die nestled safely inside it.
I hope that this book blesses you and that the exuberance with
which I write stirs your heart with a great desire to press on to
discover the abundant joy that is your birthright in Christ Jesus.

CHAPTER ONE

welcome to your heart

The spirit of bondage is gradually departing, and the hour of liberty, which he longs for, is approaching. —John Newton[1]

I fidgeted restlessly as I sat in the church sanctuary and waited for my big moment to arrive. Thoughts were racing through my mind and my heart was beating rapidly with excitement as I listened to the speaker drone on and on. I was interested in only one thing, and I was having a difficult time waiting for it.

The speaker was a good friend of mine, a young woman who I had befriended at work, and I was thrilled that she'd been asked to give her testimony at church. Heather's testimony was an exceptional story of transformation, and I had been a large part of it. When I first met Heather as a coworker in the laboratory of a big city hospital, she was almost invisible. She spoke hesitantly and quietly, her facial expressions flat and unresponsive in conversation. Heather moved slowly, every step drawn out, every action painfully sluggish as though the simplest tasks in life were a heavy burden. I felt sorry for her. She was gossiped about by other workers and mistreated by some. Since she had moved to town to take this job, she had no friends and her life seemed sad and lonely. Heather needed help: she needed Jesus, and quite clearly, *she needed me!*

Having grown up in a strong and enthusiastic missionary household, I knew exactly what God wanted me to do. He wanted me to love Heather, to become her friend, and to share the gospel with her. I got to work immediately. I had just moved back to the United States after working as a missionary in Africa and was newly married to a man who was called to the ministry and attending seminary.

Evangelism topped the list of things that I knew God required of me, and to be honest, Africa hadn't gone too well in that department. I had worked for two years in a hospital laboratory and tried hard to witness to people and disciple them, but I hadn't led anyone to the Lord. In fact, I had behaved quite badly as a young, immature twenty-one-year-old missionary and had a nagging suspicion that lots of good people had wasted a great deal of money on me. No one else knew that I thought these things about myself, but I was tormented by my failure to be a good missionary. Ministering to Heather was my chance to redeem my reputation.

Heather turned out to be an even better project than I could have imagined. She responded beautifully to all my attempts to befriend her. Soon she was a fixture in our home and began coming to church with my husband and me. When I took a new job, she followed and moved to live near us and the church we attended. She made a profession of faith and seemed to come alive before our very eyes.

Heather's story was dramatic as it involved all the worst sins that good Christians could possibly imagine, sins like sexual promiscuity and abortion. Guilt and shame had shrouded her life and body, and she had lived life in zombie mode, walking through her world shielded from the gaze of others by a portable, invisible coffin of silence. As the guilt was lifted, her countenance began to change. She talked more, became more animated, and began to smile and laugh. After a couple of years, Heather began dating a kind and gracious Christian man who proposed to her. New life took hold of her and transformed the invisible girl inside and out. This was a dramatic story, and I was the primary player on the stage of Heather's new life.

Yet as I continued to listen to Heather's lengthy narrative, I was starting to get annoyed. Heather's version of the story sounded highly inaccurate. She kept talking about God and what he had done in her life, but she hadn't mentioned my name even once. Annoyance blossomed into anger as I began to wonder if she was going to mention me at all. How on earth could she explain her story without thanking me and telling everyone how I had given my life to reach her with the gospel? Ministering to Heather had been costly to me, and surely I deserved some credit! What was more, this particular group of people had failed to be impressed by my missionary biography. They didn't particularly care that I'd gone to deepest, darkest Africa. In fact, they hadn't noticed me much at all, so I needed a little help in the notoriety department. Heather's story was finally drawing to a close, and my anger turned to fury as I realized that she had no intention of mentioning me at all. Bitter thoughts flooded my mind and I rehearsed what I would say to punish her for her foul ingratitude. I desperately hated Heather in that moment.

A MOMENT OF INSIGHT

Suddenly, out of nowhere, a thought appeared in my mind: *Barbara, you are a glory-hound and a limelight lover. This is not your story; it's mine, and all the credit and glory belong to me.* Never in my life had I had a thought quite like that before. It wasn't a voice; it was a thought, but a thought so powerful and moving that I felt suddenly swallowed up in a hot blaze of light that exposed me to the core of my soul.

I'd heard words like that before coming from the mouth of my college roommate as we competed shamelessly for the position of president of one of the evangelical Christian fellowship groups on campus. She had seen things in me to which I was utterly blind, and she chose a moment on the steps of the dining hall to drop the bombshell on me four years previously. She told me, "Barbara, you are such a limelight lover and always have to be at the center of attention." I was not rescued by a thought on that earlier day. Instead, anger rose up in me like a violent storm, and I gave my roommate a vicious shove that almost threw her down the stairway we stood upon. There was no metaphorical hot blaze of light to arrest my thoughts, only foul and bitter hatred toward a girl who would not adore me and who threatened my high view of myself.

This was completely different, however. I felt like the apostle Paul must have felt on the road to Damascus when Jesus confronted him and said, "Saul, Saul, why are you persecuting me?" (Acts 9:4). It was as if I were mentally thrown to the ground, blinded by a glory so bright that I couldn't bear it. Now the Lord was asking me, "Barbara, why are you stealing my glory?" I imagined a crushed and bleeding Jesus nailed to a cross, looking at me, knowing my thoughts, and asking, "How can you take credit for what I have done? Did you die for Heather? Did you give her faith and life? Did you open her eyes to see?" For a brief moment I felt deeply convicted, and the foulness of these sins threatened to consume me. I was shocked and undone by the ugliness of my thoughts, since I'd had no idea I was capable of such disgusting crimes against God and humanity! Yet it had been true all along! I had been sinning like this for years because my roommate had seen it clearly many years earlier.

Gradually, however, another thought dawned on me. Instead of feeling despair and rejection, I began to feel lavishly cherished. God was not at all surprised by my glory-loving, attention-seeking soul. I had been blind to the truth about myself, but Jesus had hung on that cross for *me*, for *this specific* sin. As I envisioned myself standing before a bleeding Jesus, naked, ashamed, and exposed, I expected and deserved rebuke, disappointment, and rejection from my Savior. But this was not what I was receiving. Instead, he extended love, compassion, and infinite patience with my brokenness and weakness. I felt loved and treasured by God even though nothing had yet changed in me. I was a prideful Pharisee at that very moment, and in many ways I still am. On that day sorrow and gratitude rushed through my heart together as joyful companions for the first time. I responded, "Lord, I am so sorry that I am eager to steal your glory; it is true that this is really who I am. Thank you for loving me and forgiving me in the face of such treason." Until that time I had always believed that God was lucky to have me on his side. Now I finally saw myself as a bitter enemy whom God had chosen to love and welcome as a precious child. For the first time in my life, grace looked and felt amazing, completely unexpected in light of my rebellious behavior toward God.

It would be years before I would understand what happened on that day. The Holy Spirit was beginning to open my eyes to see myself more clearly in order to free me from bondage to myself! Truth was starting to replace self-deception, and conviction was beginning to feel sweet instead of simply bitter and humiliating.

But those good and true thoughts were for a later time, because shame and embarrassment ruled this particular evening as my apprehension of God's patient love faded away. My roommate had been right about me and I was mortified. Why hadn't I seen it? How could a good Christian girl from a strong missionary family be so selfish and self-glorifying? How was I capable of such deep hatred toward others who were my brothers and sisters in Christ? How could I possibly be this sinful when I'd been a Christian for more than twenty years? What was this filth pouring out of me, and how would I ever survive it?

THE ANATOMY OF THE SOUL

Have you ever asked yourself those disturbing questions? Perhaps you have seen the secret inward sins of your heart that no one else sees and wondered how you could be such a bad Christian, or whether you're a Christian at all. Perhaps you are alarmed by new patterns of sinful behavior that you see emerging now and your own powerlessness to defeat them. Do you wonder about those old sins that have been around for a long time and that you cannot conquer no matter how hard you try? I hope it will comfort you to know that you are not alone. In fact, all Christians have this problem, whether they are painfully aware of the secret sins that hold them captive or still blind to them, like I was for many years.

The predicament we all share is that while we are new creations in Christ (2 Cor. 5:17) and have been given living hearts with which to know and worship God (Ezek. 36:26–27), we are still very sinful people. We remain weak, rebellious, and inclined toward drifting away from God until the day we see him face to face. Along with the hymn writer, each one of us can say that we are "prone to wander, Lord, I feel it, prone to leave the God I love."[2]

You may not hear much teaching on this problem in our churches. Few people, and perhaps especially few pastors, are willing or able to open up their lives and hearts for public exposure and scrutiny. Most of us prefer to hide our sin and weakness instead of revealing ourselves and experiencing shame and humiliation. As a result, our churches have become places where we perform well for others and speak far more about our victories than our struggles. In consequence, many Christians wrestle with the agony of sinful failure in isolation and desperation. The silent message is deafening: Christians are people who quickly grow and change, and if you are weak and struggling you must not be a believer, or perhaps worse, you are a particularly bad Christian in whom God is very, very disappointed.

This silence has not always been the case. In particular, there was one eighteenth-century pastor who was remarkably open about the secret sins of his heart—John Newton. You may know him as the author of the famous hymn "Amazing Grace."

John Newton was born in 1725, and for the first six years of his life he benefited from the love and teaching of his mother. She was a devout Christian who faithfully taught him God's Word and filled his young mind with psalms, hymns, and teachings from historic catechisms. When she died John was left to the care of his father, who was a moral man but had no faith in God or interest in religion. At the tender age of eleven, he found himself working on a ship for the first time and keeping company with other rough sailors.

Newton soon became a young man who could swear and blaspheme like the rest of the crew. He took perverse joy in profaning the name of God and in stirring up trouble and chaos wherever he could. Despite many attempts at moral reform, it would be another eleven years before he was converted. He would go on to describe himself as one whom God rescued against his own will.

During his sailing career, Newton was involved in the slave trade and captained several vessels on voyages to pick up fresh cargo in Africa. Although he was not immediately convicted of the perversity of the slave trade at the time of salvation, he held distaste for this occupation that required chains and shackles. Eventually, health problems forced him to abandon life aboard ship and settle into a more stable job as surveyor of the tide pools in Liverpool. Newton's mother had predicted and hoped that he would one day be set apart for the ordained ministry of the Word of God, but Newton barely dared to hope that one who had been as sinful and perverse as he had been could ever be given such a privilege. Yet this is exactly what God did.

After several years of growth and training under godly evangelical ministers, both inside and outside the Church of England, Newton was accepted as a minister in the established church and was made vicar of a church in Olney, where he served for many years before moving to London. He became known for his pastor's heart and his great skill in counseling the large numbers of people who came to him—or wrote to him—for advice. Through years of ministering to people in every stage of life, Newton became an expert on "the anatomy of the soul" and took particular interest and joy in studying the progressive work of spiritual growth in believers, what theologians call "sanctification." Newton was captivated by what God teaches his children through the complex process of sinners maturing in grace from the time of salvation onward.

Excellent books have been written on the subject of sanctification, yet Newton's work stands above the rest for one simple and (to us) shocking reason. He was open about the fact that he was still a wretched sinner long after he became a Christian. Many believers are willing and eager to talk about what big sinners they were before they were saved, but few invite you into their hearts to see what huge sinners they still are now. This is risky stuff. People might look down on you and reject you if you do that. They might not come to your church or listen to your sermons. They might trash your reputation and gossip about you. These dangers are indeed real. However, Newton had such great confidence in the love of God for him and such a great love for those he counseled that he refused to participate in the conspiracy of silence. He would not allow other believers to think more highly of him than they ought to think.

From his tremendous knowledge of Scripture, his vast experience as a sinner himself, and his service as a pastor of sinners, John Newton noticed that God is up to something purposeful and specific in the hearts of those he saves. If you were to ask

Christians around the world what God wants from the people he has saved, most would probably answer "obedience." There is great truth in that answer, but it is not enough. If the sovereign God's primary goal in sanctifying believers is simply to make us more holy, it is hard to explain why most of us make only "small beginnings" on the road to personal holiness in this life, as the Heidelberg Catechism puts it (see Catechism Q. 113). In reality, God wants something much more precious in our lives than mere outward conformity to his will. After all, obedience is tricky business and can be confusing to us. We can be obedient outwardly while sinning wildly on the inside, as the example of the Pharisees makes clear. In fact, many of my worst sins have been committed in the context of my best obedience. Before the night of Heather's testimony, I saw my relationship to her as a loving mentor to a young convert. Much of my behavior toward Heather was exactly how I should have acted. However, I was also a judgmental, self-righteous, and entitled Pharisee who craved recognition for all that I had done. My outward obedience actually became the framework and context for my inward sin.

In the same way, when we witness to unbelievers, we are obeying God. Yet if we are full of pride as we do it, looking down on those who find it difficult to witness and don't do it, we can be sinning even while we're obeying. If we think that the person who is rejecting the gospel is doing so because they are less intelligent or morally inferior to us, we are sinning. If we take credit for the new life of faith that only God can give, we are sinning. Christians thus face a seriously disturbing predicament: when we are most successful in obeying God, we so often also hear that whisper of self-exaltation and superiority. We cannot escape it. If this is true of us even in our best moments, what hope is there for us in the race toward true holiness that changes us inside and out?

John Newton teaches us, however, that God's goal in our sanctification is not merely better obedience and increasing sinlessness. He observes that if God had wanted to do so, he could have made us instantaneously perfect at the moment of our salvation. After all, we know that he will make us instantly perfect when we die or when he comes again, and since all things are equally easy to the all-powerful God, he could as readily have sanctified us completely the moment we were saved.

Let's be honest: if the chief work of the Holy Spirit in sanctification is to make Christians more sin-free, then he isn't doing a very good job. The church throughout the ages and throughout the world has not usually been known for its purity and goodness. Instead, it is wracked by a constant history of strife, violence, and hypocrisy. People often cannot differentiate a believer from an unbeliever by their apparent goodness. In fact, there are many unbelievers who are morally superior to Christians and live lives of far greater nobility, generosity, and purpose than we who profess faith in Christ.

God could have saved us and made us instantly perfect. Instead, he chose to save us and leave indwelling sin in our hearts and bodies to wage war against the new and blossoming desires to please God that accompany salvation. This is a raging battle that we often lose, and that often leaves us feeling defeated and joyless in our walk with God. Yet Newton also points out that since we know God does all things for his own glory and the good of his people, his decision to leave Christians with many struggles with sin must also somehow serve to glorify him and benefit his people. This is shocking news, isn't it?

Think of what this means. God thinks that you will actually come to know and love him better as a desperate and weak sinner in continual need of grace than you would as a triumphant Christian warrior who wins each and every battle against sin. This makes sense out of our experience as Christians. If the job

of the Holy Spirit is to make you more humble and dependent
on Christ, more grateful for his sacrifice and more adoring of
him as a wonderful Savior, then he might be doing a very, very
good job even though you still sin every day.

WHY IT MATTERS

What difference does it make whether you believe that Christians should go from strength to strength and live victorious lives of obedience, or whether you believe that Christians will remain on earth in a state of great weakness and utter dependence on God for every single good thought? *It makes all the difference in the world.* It matters immensely what you believe about yourself and about God. It matters that you have a true and accurate assessment of who you are as a believer before God, what God expects from you, and what you should expect from yourself. It matters a great deal that you understand what the Holy Spirit is up to in your life and how he does his work. Jesus invited us to live lives of joy and rest at the same time as we pursue the hard work of striving to obey God and grow in holiness (Matt. 11:28–30). I know many Christians who are trying hard to be holy, but few who are able to balance that hard work with joyful resting at the same time.

If you are a discouraged Christian who is surprised by your sin and sure that God is disappointed with you, then you need truth from God's Word to free you from the emotional roller coaster ride of your successes and failures. If you are a proud Christian who feels better than others because of your many strengths and triumphs, you need God's Spirit to show you the truth about your heart and humble you. If your peace now rests in what you are able to do, then where will you turn when you fall and commit sins that you never dreamed you could? On that day, you will need to know this truth to survive your failure and rejoice in the middle of it. Whoever you are and whatever spiritual state you find yourself in, I urge you not to give up on finding your joy *in Christ* in this life. Sinless perfection and complete peace and joy must wait for heaven, but abundant joy here and now in Christ is your birthright and your inheritance, even when you sin and fail miserably to be a good Christian.

John Newton shows us from Scripture that true sanctification is all about growing in humility, dependence, and gratitude. Joy blossoms in our hearts not as we try harder and harder to grow, but as we see more clearly the depths of our sin and understand more fully our utter helplessness. Only then will we take our eyes off ourselves and look to Christ for all that we need in life and in death. Only then will we truly cherish our Savior and believe that we need him every minute of every day, and that without him we can do nothing (John 15:5).

Newton also demonstrates that God has some surprising ways of freeing his people from the bondage of their own performance and leading them to the joy and freedom of resting in Christ alone. If it is true that "the heart is deceitful above all things, and desperately wicked" (Jer. 17:9 KJV) and that we will continue to struggle with our depraved hearts throughout our lives, our ongoing sin can actually be the means God uses to glorify himself even while humbling us.

What if God chooses to glorify himself as much in our sinful failure, by bearing with us patiently, as he does by demonstrating his power to change us and strengthen us for obedience? What if sin continues to have victory over our best intentions many times each day? Is it possible for us to have profound joy even when we find ourselves sinning a great deal? We will investigate these important questions in this book, in order to understand ourselves and God's way of working in this world and in our hearts individually. We will begin our exploration by observing John Newton's description of the three stages of Christian growth and by noticing *what* God does in each stage and *how* he does it. Buckle up, my friends—there is serious joy ahead!

FOR FURTHER REFLECTION

1. What did you expect that growth as a Christian would look and feel like when you were first saved? How would you describe the way in which your growth has taken place?

2. Do you secretly consider yourself better or worse than other Christians? Why?

3. Are you shocked by the sin you still see in your heart and actions? Why or why not?

4. In what new ways have you been seeing patterns of sin that have actually been around for a long time?

5. Do you tend to share your sinful failure with other believers, or do you tend to hide it and cover it up? Why?

6. What do you think God's goal is in sanctifying you?

babes in Christ

*While he is thus young in the knowledge of the gospel . . .
the Lord is pleased to favor him with cordials that he
may not be swallowed up with over-much sorrow.*
—John Newton[1]

John Newton often expressed a special love and affection for new believers in Christ. He observed their passion and zeal for God and recalled his own story and the warm feelings that accompanied the earliest days of his spiritual walk. Unlike many of us, John Newton clearly remembered the day God opened his eyes and gave him the gift of faith. He was a young sailor, only twenty-three years old, but he had already spent many years in a state of flagrant rebellion against God. In his early childhood Newton had been raised by a godly mother who taught him biblical doctrine and modeled a deep and genuine love for God. Newton says of his mother, "She stored my memory with many valuable pieces, chapters and portions of Scripture, catechisms, hymns and poems."[2] However, following her death when he was just six years old, he was left in the care of a father who taught him morality, but did not continue his Christian education. It would be many years before God took the doctrines his mother had taught him and pressed them deep into his heart.

In between the time of his mother's death and his new birth, Newton became a sailor and a brazen rebel against God. He referred to himself as a high-handed sinner who delighted in mischief, blasphemy, and what he called "abominable frolics."[3] He treated himself to every kind of bodily pleasure, with only one exception. Though he enjoyed inciting others to drunkenness, he didn't particularly enjoy alcohol. Newton made several attempts to reform during his wild and licentious years, but they were primarily conducted through extreme efforts to control his outward behavior. He would spend hours reading his Bible and other religious books and denying himself worldly pleasure. However, his efforts at reform never lasted, and each attempt was followed by a relapse into deeper sin than before. At times he struggled with despair and depression, and on several occasions he even tried to take his own life. Many years later Newton would conclude that God had lovingly spared and rescued him, much against his own will. He went on to describe himself as a "monument to grace" and a trophy of God's power to change hearts. Newton was persuaded that one reason God had saved him was just to prove that he could![4]

March 21, 1748, was a day that Newton always commemorated. He wrote in his autobiography, "On that day the Lord sent from on high and delivered me out of deep waters."[5] It was the day when the ship on which he was traveling as a passenger sailed to safety after four weeks of harrowing storms and near-death escapes. It was also the day when his spiritual eyes were opened and he was given just enough faith to hope that God might love and save *him*. Although it would be a long time before he would enjoy assurance of his salvation, Newton looked back on this season of his life with sentimentality.

He was soon granted a great desire to pray, read Scripture, and listen to the preaching of God's Word. These are the "cordials," or special gifts, that he believed God often gives to young converts to encourage them to press on. Because they are immature and fearful, the Lord "gathers the lambs in his arms, and carries them in his bosom,"[6] granting them extra measures of enthusiastic desire, success in spiritual discipline, and protection from Satan. As Newton went on to grow in grace and became a skilled pastor, counselor, and hymn writer, he reflected that, in spite of their many weaknesses, new believers' passion and zeal were attributes to be admired and respected.

WARM HEART, WEAK FAITH

During his many years of pastoral work, Newton noticed that the life of the baby Christian is experienced primarily in the realm of feelings rather than in the realm of knowledge. His "faith is weak, but his heart is warm."[7] He tends to mistake the nature of these gifts from God and think they are his, however. Although they are given by God and meant for his comfort, the baby Christian rests in these early feelings and successes and thinks that he will always have them. He believes that he is right and strong because he has them, and he is prone to feeling superior to believers that don't.

Newton observed that, like Israel on the banks of the Red Sea, the immature Christian thinks that his troubles are now over. The strong arm of God has parted the seas for him and led him to safety, and he presumes that it will always be so. He thinks that there is nothing left now but to walk through life with the victorious hand of God on his side, and then to enter heaven forever. He doesn't yet know that, like Israel, there is a huge desert to cross before entering the Promised Land. The desert he has yet to see and grapple with properly is the wilderness of his own sinful heart.

In all his teaching on Christian growth, Newton emphasizes the fact that no two people have exactly the same story. The Lord's specific method and means of calling souls to faith, as well as that of carrying out the subsequent work of grace in their lives, are as varied and unique as each individual Christian. However, he argues that the content of *what* God is teaching them and the *process* by which he teaches them are the same for every Christian. We all need to learn complete dependence on Christ, for without him we can do nothing. What is more, God teaches this truth to us by means of experience. We will discuss both of these things in depth later on. For now, we'll just consider the impact that inexperience and lack of knowledge have on the young Christian.

Newton argues that to become a Christian a person must understand in some way that he is a sinner, but at the same time he does not and cannot know immediately the depth of depravity that remains within him. Therefore, he typically expects too much of himself as he aims at obedience. To be sure, sometimes God gives a person extraordinary strength and grace at the time of salvation. I know of people who have accepted Christ and immediately given up addictions to alcohol, foul language, sex, cigarettes, and food. John Newton stopped using blasphemy and bad language almost immediately after he was saved. It is easy to see how this experience could be confusing, however. Baby Christians tend to be utterly amazed at such power and conclude that God will always do this for them if they ask, or if they just try hard enough. After all, if God could deliver them from something that held them in bondage for so long, something that they have tried over and over again in vain to defeat, it would be natural to think that God would continue to display this kind of grace in their lives all the time.

Young believers may also be prone to thinking they had something significant to do with the change process themselves. They might reason that God gave them this gift because they prayed a lot, read the Bible, or attended church faithfully. Since God hates sin and teaches his children to hate it, they may assume that

God will quickly obliterate sin from their lives. Such experiences make them hopeful, joyful, and extremely confident.

These immature believers may also become judgmental toward other Christians.[8] Because a legalistic attitude still clings to them and they do not yet understand the character of God, they are prone to rebuking and censuring people who express weakness and struggles with sin. They have known victory and cannot imagine anything else, until God, in his kindness, initiates the next phase of their growth in grace. This growth does not happen all at once, nor is there a prescribed time frame for any phase. In fact, even people who have grown to maturity in Christ will at times revert to this childlike behavior.

Yet there is a general progression by which the Lord leads his people. The young and zealous convert one day finds that his comforts are withdrawn: he finds that he has no heart to pray, no appetite for reading God's word, and no desire to attend church. Indwelling sin revives with fresh strength, and Satan is permitted to return and tempt him with greater strength and rage. As a result, the young Christian often becomes discouraged and downcast, thinking that God has abandoned him and that perhaps he might not be a Christian at all. Some people might call this "backsliding," but Newton contends that God is actually leading the young Christian forward in his walk with Christ. It will be for his own good and for the glory of God for this baby Christian to discover his own weakness and his need for the righteousness of Christ. In love, God will crush his growing spiritual pride and lead him to a deeper and richer understanding of the covenant of grace.

Because the law of God is written on his heart and the gospel has not yet sunk in deeply, the baby Christian gravitates toward those Scriptures that tell him what to do, and there are many. He loves God and knows that those who love God obey him (John 14:15), and he eagerly desires to know how to please God with his actions. He does not know the whole counsel of God's Word or understand that the greatest heroes of Scripture are deeply flawed throughout their lives. He reads of Paul's weakness but does not know what to make of it. Like a little baby who crawls forth into his world to discover what he can and cannot do, and what he may and may not do, the young believer sets forth with enthusiasm and optimism as he reads the Bible and plans to obey God well.

Another characteristic of those young in faith is that they are prone to enormous spiritual ups and downs. Baby Christians feel more than they think, and their feelings often depend on how well they are doing in the realm of obedience. The judgmental spirit in which they evaluate others often carries over to the way they evaluate themselves. When they succeed in their religious disciplines, they think that God takes more delight in them than when they fail. When they begin to glimpse weakness in their own lives, they respond with elaborate strategies to turn over a new leaf and try harder to combat whatever is troubling them.

My husband pastors many college students, and almost every week we hear of new and extreme answers to the problem of spiritual failure. There are all-night prayer vigils and a wide variety of cleansing fasts designed to guarantee spiritual victory and growth. There are Bible-reading programs, retreats, and devotional studies promoting self-denial and greater discipline as a pathway to better obedience. These young men and women long to feel good about themselves and to know that God is happy with them.

I have always called Robbie, our fourth child, my sunshine boy. He was born with strawberry blond hair, a dimple in his cheek, and an affinity for people. His smile could take your breath away. It seemed that each and every time we looked at him, he beamed with delight and the sheer joy of connecting eye to eye with someone. His grin was irresistible, and as a result he drew many admirers. He was born into the chaos of our first church plant, and it was a blessing that so many people lined up on Sundays for a chance to hold him and enjoy him.

Rob grew into a sensitive toddler who craved the approval of his parents. This was great because it meant I rarely had to discipline him! He was a little boy who needed to know that we loved him, and the few times I do remember swatting his little behind seemed especially painful to him. On one occasion I had to spank him, and since I was habitually overwhelmed by the needs and naughtiness of four other young children, I sent him to his room to sit on his bed until I could talk to him. Before long I heard a pathetic little voice calling out in despair, "I'll behave now! I'll behave now!" This little man desperately wanted to be restored to the smiles of approval that he so enjoyed, and his solution was to promise to obey if I would let him out of his jail cell.

Baby Christians are a lot like that little boy who was desperate to know that he was loved in spite of his naughtiness. They cannot yet imagine that their heavenly Father could always be pleased with them because of Christ's obedience in their place (an idea I will discuss in more detail in chapter 12), so they eagerly seek to win his approval through their own compliance. They will go to great lengths to pursue a feeling of security in knowing that they can please God, so they make promises of obedience to him that they could never keep. But God is far too kind to let them find rest in their performance for long.

In his reflections on this early stage of growth, John Newton calls this period springtime with the young convert, who is in full bloom. [9] He is not yet bearing the autumn fruits of habitual repentance and dependence on God alone for his salvation, but he is flowering and that fruit will surely come in season. His knowledge of God and of himself is small, but it is growing every day. The Lord is slowly delivering him from the love of sin and setting his desires supremely on Jesus Christ. Though his emotions are held captive by his spiritual performance, the hour of freedom is approaching. He rightly longs for joy in God, and it is on the way. By a deeper discovery of the gospel he will soon come to trust more fully in God's acceptance of him and rest on the finished work of Christ.

PRACTICAL IMPLICATIONS

Newton's insightful analysis of the characteristics of baby believers is extremely helpful. It can be an encouraging marker of growth when we can look back and see how God has changed us and steadied us in faith. I myself can look back and remember what it felt like to be wildly overconfident and presumptuous about my own spiritual growth. Perhaps I spent more than the average amount of time in the earliest phase of growth! When I was in high school, I witnessed boldly to everyone at my public high school, teachers and students alike. I thought that God would be proud of me, and I was determined to earn some stars for my crown. I didn't manage to lead many people to Christ, but I eagerly took credit for those that I did. I had little knowledge and truly believed that it was up to me to persuade people to believe. As you can perhaps imagine, this led to aggressive, obnoxious, and desperate behavior on my part! I took it badly when people rejected what I said, and I got depressed when I failed in my mission. I honestly thought that it was entirely my fault that they were going to hell. I was sure that God was deeply disappointed in my failures, so I tried harder. I can look back now and see that I didn't know much about God, or about the sinful motivations I had for evangelism.

My mood rose and fell according to my successes and failures in this and many other avenues of obedience. These things didn't begin to change in me until the first year of my marriage, when God kindly began to open my eyes. It can be exciting and hopeful to look back over many years and see that God has been hard at work, and that I am not the same person that I was back then.

It is also helpful to understand where other believers are in their walk with the Lord. When I teach women's Bible studies, I minister to women of all ages. It is a common occurrence to have someone in the group confess their struggle and weakness in a certain area, only to be rebuked and censured by a younger sister in Christ, who eagerly shares three easy ways they can overcome their problem. The legalistic spirit of a young believer is revealed by phrases like, "If I could lose weight, then anyone can. Just do what I did!" or "Quitting cigarettes is easy when you trust God," or "Just ask Jesus to help you every time you feel angry and he will take the feeling away." One young woman thought she was helping me in my struggle with obesity when she said, "All I did was pray every time I put food in my mouth, and I lost 100 pounds! I'm sure this will work for you too if you will just discipline yourself to do it." Instead of feeling encouraged, I felt more defeated than ever! Now I would somehow have to remember to pray every time I shoveled food into my mouth, and I knew I wasn't up for the task.

Simplistic answers to complex problems can be discouraging to weary strugglers, and downright annoying at times. In reaction I have sometimes been guilty of discouraging baby Christians by popping their bubble and rubbing their noses in the long and difficult path that lies ahead, instead of seeking to understand their hearts and encourage them in what God is doing in their lives presently. If God has given them unusual success in some area of their lives, that is something wonderful to be celebrated and not sneered at. It may be true that within a few months or years they will find their comforts withdrawn. If so, God will walk them through that in his time and he doesn't need me to belittle his current actions in order to warn them about what he will most likely do in the future. God's timetable isn't mine;

it's better than mine! Understanding Newton's stages of growth has helped me to become more patient with young believers and gentler in my speech toward them.

We can't help but compare ourselves to others, and others to one another. Unfortunately, we frequently use these observations to feel superior or inferior to people around us. We should therefore practice great caution in evaluating the spiritual maturity of people around us. We can, and at times do, use this information to judge and demean others, or we can use it to love and encourage.

Nevertheless, the circumstances and shaping influences that accompany an individual's profession of faith matter a great deal in the progress of his growth in Christ. God not only determines whom he will draw to himself, but he governs all of the circumstances and situations from which he calls each one, as well as the settings in which they will grow.

A TALE OF TWO CHRISTIANS

We have seen God's sovereign control at work in the lives of two individuals who came to faith through churches in which we have worked. Ginny became a Christian through our first church plant in a poor community on the outskirts of Oxford, England. Like most of the people to whom we ministered, she was functionally illiterate, unemployed, and before she met us had never been to church or had significant contact with Christians. She lived alone with her two children, dependent upon welfare for her support, and was diffident and shy. Ginny might never be able to read the Bible for herself, let alone study theology or mine the wonderful depths of the doctrines of God. Yet she is nonetheless a trophy of grace, as surely saved as the most knowledgeable pastor or theologian. Even though Ginny may live many years as a believer and still remain immature and young in the faith, she is a shining beacon glowing brightly in a dark world, loudly proclaiming God's power to save and preserve all whom he has chosen through a variety of life circumstances.

Others come to faith surrounded by many of life's richest blessings. Several months ago a young man began attending our new church plant because he was smitten with our daughter. At the time she returned his attentions, and we assumed his interest in being with us on Sundays was more romantic than spiritual. Nevertheless, we prayed for him often and watched him closely. This remarkable young man was academically brilliant and highly motivated toward success. He was at the top of his high school graduating class and planning to study chemical engineering at a large university. He was handsome, articulate, winsome, and strongly gifted in a variety of ways.

When he attended our church he encountered a congregation that was bursting with sharp college students who were on fire with the desire to know and serve God. They were quite the role models. Most of the preachers he heard were ordained ministers who were also professors of biblical and theological studies, each highly educated and strongly gifted in explaining and applying God's word. As we watched him each week we noticed that he was singing enthusiastically and was deeply moved by the confession of sin and assurance of pardon in each service.

After a few months, our daughter and this young man lost interest in each other, and we feared that he would fall away completely and we would never see him again. Yet he came back week after week. He read his Bible voraciously and devoured every book my husband recommended. He asked questions and thought deeply about our answers. It wasn't long before he made a clear profession of a vibrant faith in Jesus Christ, and on Easter Sunday of that year he was baptized, joined the church, and participated in the Lord's Supper for the first time. Tears of wonder and gratitude streamed down my face as my son passed the elements to him, proclaiming joyfully, "Chris, the body of Christ is broken for you; the blood of Christ is shed for you."

Now imagine what this young man's growth in grace might look like compared to our friend in England. He is educated, gifted, and not only is he able to read, he loves reading more than almost anything else. He has easy access to understandable preaching and participates faithfully in a campus ministry at his college. As a result he is likely to grow more quickly in the faith and progress further into maturity, and at a young age surpass my less privileged friends who have known Christ for much longer. Education will never guarantee godliness, but it is certainly a wonderful asset for those in whom the Spirit is deepening the knowledge of God and understanding of his Word.

Yet at the same time, Newton explains, every believer is equally dependent on the Holy Spirit for understanding and spiritual growth. Furthermore, the Holy Spirit isn't doing exactly the same thing in the same order in the life of every Christian. Christians grow spiritually at different rates in different areas, even if they come from similar backgrounds and hear exactly the same sermons. The Holy Spirit is working out *his* perfect will in sanctifying each of us, and this doesn't always look the way we think it should.

What is your salvation story? Our stories are as varied and unique as we are. Some of us were raised in Christian homes and taught the Bible from our earliest days. I accepted Christ at a young age, and though I "decided to follow Jesus" about one hundred times before I was confident that I could stop going forward in church, I can barely remember a time when I didn't believe in him and trust him in some way. My brothers grew up in the same home, yet each of them has his own story of God's work in his life, at a different age and in a different way. Some of you were perhaps born into irreligious homes or religious homes where the Bible was wielded as a weapon and God's law used to frighten and intimidate. God uses all the circumstances of life to shape the trajectory of our growth in grace, including the doctrines that we adopt and the churches that we attend. He is sovereign over each and every detail that will shape the trajectory of each individual growth curve. We will not all reach the same level of maturity in Christ, nor will we all believe identical things in this life, but every one of us will live and grow under his loving care and sovereign rule.

Indeed, God nowhere promises that every believer will reach a particular measure of spiritual growth while we live here on earth. He not only gives different gifts to different Christians, he is also sovereign over the amount of faith we possess (Rom. 12:3). Some will live and die with great faith, while others—equally beloved children of God—will struggle their whole lives with faith that is weak and faint. In his great wisdom God has chosen to glorify himself through saving a church made up of believers of all ages, at all stages of maturity and immaturity, living before him with faith that may be strong or weak, according to what he has given to each one.

To summarize, then, baby Christians generally have warm and lively affections for God without a deep understanding of the sinfulness of their hearts and the character of God. They are inclined to spiritual pride when they are doing well, and to rebuking and correcting others who aren't doing quite so well. They are prone to despair and to doubt when they fall into sin. The strength of their joy rests a great deal in their feelings and not yet in their reason and understanding of the truth. Their views of God's grace are very narrow, and they are persuaded that God loves them and is proud of them when they stand strong, but fear that God will punish and abandon them when they sin.

47

GOOD NEWS FOR BABY CHRISTIANS

So what are you to do if you are reading this and you begin to suspect that you are still a baby Christian and not quite as mature as you thought? Should you be discouraged? What if this chapter describes someone you are mentoring or sounds like your spouse, your children, your parents, or even your pastor? Should you panic? John Newton's answer is, "Absolutely not!" His calm and steady assertion that the God who began a good work in each Christian will carry it on to the day of completion (Phil. 1:6) is an enormous source of comfort and relief. Spiritual growth to maturity is God's work from beginning to end, and he alone will get the credit. The same God who made the universe out of nothing and who counts the hairs on your head will have his way with you in all things. He does not ordain the beginning and the end of your story only to leave the middle part—your life as a believer here on earth—up to you! That means that, at this very moment, you are exactly as holy and mature in your faith as God wants you to be. He cannot be disappointed in you or surprised by you if he is the one controlling the entire process of growth from start to finish. Furthermore, all the people whom you love and wish were more mature are also exactly where God wants them to be right now. He always gets his way and you cannot stop him!

Praise God for this good news! Contrary to popular belief, our spiritual growth is not up to us, nor is the spiritual growth of the people around us. This misunderstanding can lead us to much inward anxiety and even abusive behavior if we try to force people to understand truths that they are not ready to hear. We need to listen carefully to people's stories and seek to discern what God is and isn't doing in them rather than attempt to force them to achieve instant maturity.

When I seek to teach biblical principles to a group of people, inevitably some will latch onto the new truth and seem to come alive, while others will continue to look at me with disbelief and doubt stamped on every feature. This is not because some of them are smart while others are dumb. Nor is it because some are more willing to learn and submit to God than others. We are all stubborn and rebellious sheep who continue to demand our own way, even after we are saved. Rather, it is because God is up to something different in each one, working according to his timetable and not mine—or theirs. Each one is equally dependent on the Holy Spirit for insight, as well as the specific desire to obey God and the ability to actually do it. We cannot change our own hearts, but neither can we resist the change that God is determined to accomplish in us.

I have often had the amazing privilege of hearing years later from the women who once thought I was crazy. They say something like this: "I heard you say this in Bible study two years ago, and at the time it didn't make any sense to me. I thought you were silly or deceived, but now I understand what you were saying because God has shown me this recently." Although I am often tempted to feel chastised for my inability to teach at these moments, I know that another principle is also at work. The Lord was waiting for a later time to teach this woman that particular truth, and he chose to get it across to her in a different way. It is all about him, all the time.

These are truths that lead to joy and freedom. It may seem great to believe that our growth is up to us when things are going well in our spiritual lives, but it is a terrifying thought when our comforts are withdrawn and we find ourselves failing and falling into sin, even though we are trying every bit as hard to obey as we were earlier. It is when we are truly at our wits' end that we are ready to learn something new about ourselves and God.

As Newton makes clear, the rate of our spiritual growth rests entirely in the hands of the Holy Spirit. Far from making us passive or uncaring about our spiritual progress, this truth actually energizes us for the struggle. After all, if you as a believer are indwelt by the Holy Spirit of the living God, you have no choice but to change and grow according to his good pleasure. Now that's good news!

FOR FURTHER REFLECTION

1. How did the circumstances surrounding your salvation affect your growth as a Christian? What special "cordials" or sweet gifts did God give to you when you were a baby in the faith?

2. Have you felt a change in your walk with the Lord in a way that reading the Bible, praying, and attending church have become more difficult for you or even undesirable? Describe when and why this happened.

3. How do you think God feels about you when you don't read the Bible and pray, or when you read and pray but your heart is out of line?

4. What does God think of you when you try hard to obey and succeed?

5. Do you think God is disappointed in you and expects you to be much further along in your growth than you are? Why or why not?

6. Do you know many people who are babies in Christ as Newton describes them? What are they like? How do you feel about them?

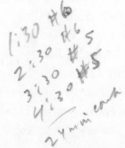

CHAPTER THREE

maturing in faith

*The characteristic of the state of [the maturing
believer] is conflict.* —John Newton[1]

What is it that marks out our growth as Christians?

While acknowledging that God's work in the individual lives
of his children is varied and unique, Newton considered it a
certain fact that God was hard at work in each one and that the
resulting fruit would be noticeable. Because Scripture frequently
compares the growth of the kingdom to the maturation process
of plants, Newton extrapolated the characteristics of the physical
growth of plants to spiritual growth in believers. Using Jesus'
parable in Mark 4:26–28, he compared the baby Christian to
young grain still in the blade, the maturing Christian to grain
that is beginning to form in the ear, and the mature Christian
to the fully developed grain. This is the perfect analogy for sanctification because maturation for plants and people is generally
slow and progressive, yet in the end it always produces fruit. Yet
we can sometimes be confused about what that fruit is meant
to look like.

For Newton, that noticeable fruit was not necessarily to
be seen so much in the realm of outward obedience as it was
in terms of the "assurance of faith," a believer's certainty that

Christ died for them and for their specific sins and not merely for sins in general. Newton concluded that though assurance was not necessary to prove that salvation had taken place, it was the key evidence of a growing and more established faith. Out of his extensive pastoral experience, he observed that one mark of a Christian moving from infanthood to greater maturity was a work of the Holy Spirit within the believer that enabled them to stop doubting their salvation when they sinned and trust more fully in the finished work of Christ on their behalf. [2] He also believed that the richest fruit of God's work in our hearts would be evidenced by increasing humility and dependence on Christ for everything, rather than in a "victorious Christian life."

For that reason, Newton did not point Christians to their own performance for comfort and assurance. Although Newton was adept at identifying the work of the Holy Spirit and eager to celebrate the resulting fruit, he constantly pointed those whom he counseled to Christ as their only hope in life and death. He expected and was confident that a person who is indwelt by the Holy Spirit of the living God was inevitably bound to change according to God's will. Like Martin Luther before him, Newton recognized that true faith is always a "living, creative, active, and powerful thing."[3] When the Holy Spirit brings a soul to life, he also begins changing that soul and, though he operates on no timetable but his own, his work must and will become evident over the course of time. Newton's views on what that fruit would look like are different than many modern thoughts on the subject, as we shall see.

Newton's view of sanctification rested entirely on God's sustaining power. As Jesus says in the parable of the vine and the branches in John 15, "apart from me you can do nothing" (v. 5).[4] Every Christian, whatever their age or stage of spiritual growth, remains as completely dependent on the Holy Spirit for both the will and the ability to obey God as the new convert is for faith

52

itself. Yet at the same time, any true branch cannot help but bear fruit as the life of the vine flows through it and as the divine vinedresser prunes it and cares for it (v. 1). Indeed, a key part of that maturing fruit is itself an ever-deepening awareness of the branch's utter dependence upon the vine moment by moment.

As a result of these twin perspectives—that we can do nothing without God's strengthening power and that God is always sovereignly at work in the believer's life—Newton had no problem urging Christians strongly toward obedience while acknowledging that without the specific work of the Holy Spirit giving them the will and the power to obey, they would fail every time.

THE ROLE OF CONFLICT

How does God free us from a young and legalistic spirit that takes pride in its performance? How does he enable us instead to set our hearts more and more completely on the finished work of Christ? Newton's answer was that God has ordained that we usually learn about the depravity of our hearts and the vastness of God's grace by experience. He laments that if we could actually understand and maintain an accurate view of ourselves from what we read in Scripture, we would be saved from a great deal of sorrow and pain. However, Newton comments, "Experience is the Lord's school, and they who are taught by him usually learn that they have no wisdom by the mistakes they make, and that they have no strength by the slips and falls they meet with."[5]

That was certainly the experience of the Israelites.[6] Like Newton's description of the young believer, the Israelites must have experienced a period of excitement and adventure when they saw God inflict plagues on the Egyptians and part the Red Sea in front of them. They experienced God's presence with them in dramatic and undeniable ways. God could easily have led them straight into the Promised Land, giving them the faithful hearts they needed to enter and conquer it. Instead, they spent forty long and painful years wandering in the wilderness. They could never have expected such an experience when God walked them through the Red Sea and destroyed Pharaoh's army, but it pleased God to set them on a pathway of adversity to show them what was in their hearts. This period captures exactly Newton's description of the life of the maturing believer: a wilderness of conflict in which the sinfulness of our hearts is repeatedly and lovingly exposed by God.

When God walks us into the wilderness of temptation and sin, we learn what we are really like. Because of our depraved natures, we are equally capable of warping God's best gifts with our idolatries as we are of despising him in times of barren dryness. Wilderness experiences are times of genuine need, sorrow, suffering, and pain that tempt us to complain against God and turn away from him. When difficulties overwhelm us, we find it hard to remember what God has done for us in the past and trust him with the present and future.

MARAH

The Israelites faced trouble remarkably quickly in the wilderness. Just three days after their great deliverance from Egypt, they ran out of water (Ex. 15:22). This was no small matter for a large group of people seeking to cross a desert. Anyone would be shaken by such a dilemma, especially when so many human lives were at stake. Relief must have flooded their minds and hearts when the pool at Marah came into view. They must have rejoiced and thanked God as they ran toward the water and began to drink thirstily. Yet when they tasted the water at Marah, they discovered to their horror that it was bitter and undrinkable. What must it have felt like to be that thirsty and to take a huge gulp of foul and bitter undrinkable water?

How do you think you would have responded? I know how I would have reacted: I would have been angry with Moses for his lousy leadership and angry with God for teasing and tormenting me, for failing to meet my needs at the time and in the way I wished. I have lived with my heart for a long time, and I have come to know its ways well! The Israelites also grumbled against Moses, and God responded graciously to their sin by giving Moses the remedy (Ex. 15:25). God wanted the Israelites, and us, to see how quickly they would forget about his miraculous and delivering love and turn on him in fear.

Imagine for a moment that we could take camera crews to the banks of the Red Sea and interview a few of the Israelites right after the Egyptians were drowned. "Excuse me, sir," we might say, "how has this miraculous event changed your view of God?" Surely some, or even most, would have said something like this: "I thought that God had forgotten and abandoned us, but now I know he is on our side." We might probe a little further and say, "Do you think you will ever, in a million years, be able to forget this amazing event?" And they would surely answer, "How could I ever forget what God has done for us tonight!" But they did forget, rather quickly. And so do we! *Reality*

At Marah, Moses threw the log into the water, the water became sweet, and all was well once again. This story ends with God's promise not to inflict the plagues of Egypt on Israel if they would listen diligently to his voice and do what is right, keeping his commandments, "for I am the LORD, your healer" (Ex. 15:26). We marvel at God's patience and love as he led them on from Marah to Elim, the wonderful place of twelve springs and seventy palm trees, a place of abundance and relief (Ex. 15:27)! Instead of punishing the Israelites for their grumbling and lack of faith, he gave them a luxurious vacation.

Yet just a few weeks after leaving the extravagant and lush oasis of Elim, the Israelites were grumbling against Moses and Aaron again and longing for the food that they had left behind in Egypt (Ex. 16). The situation would almost be laughable, if only it weren't so sad and so true of us as well. God had moved powerfully to deliver the Israelites from cruel and oppressive bondage, in which they were slaves and their babies were being murdered. Yet they quickly forgot the misery of their bondage and remembered only what they craved at the time and did not have. God sent them manna, and they loved it for a while—until they grew tired of it and complained (Num. 11:4). Then God sent them an abundance of quail, and they loved it until they hated it (Num. 11:19–20).

Sometimes God shows us our hearts by giving us what we want. I always wanted a large family. I had a strong baby addiction from an early age, and even as a single missionary was temporarily adopting abandoned babies and caring for them until permanent families could be found. When I got married, I desperately wanted children right away and pestered my husband often to "let God decide" the matter. I was a good Presbyterian and knew how to work the system! My husband was in seminary at the time and wanted to wait, but after two years he kindly reconsidered and it wasn't long before I was pregnant. I loved having babies! I was deeply gratified by motherhood as my idolatries were blessed time and time again. I loved being the center of the world for my kids. I was good at figuring out the mysteries of newborn souls, and I loved the process of watching growth take place. I loved almost every single thing about mothering, so baby followed baby at a rapid pace. I would actually be planning the next pregnancy within hours of delivering a baby. Surely this was madness!

It wasn't until our fifth and youngest child started school that the gravity of the situation began to dawn on me and I started to wonder what on earth we had done. I was overwhelmed with having to homeschool so many children because the public schools in our area were not satisfactory and we couldn't afford private education. I was overwhelmed with laundry and cooking and with the emotional, spiritual, and educational needs of this growing pack of children. I began to realize what a ridiculous, arrogant, and overconfident fool I had been to ever think I could parent so many children well. The wilderness of exhausting demands was revealing my selfishness, foolishness, pride, and weakness, and I was not a happy camper. God lovingly crushed my pride and overconfidence by giving me an abundance of what I had so desperately craved, and he showed me how I would need his grace moment by moment to survive his generous answer to my requests.

At other times, like the Israelites at Marah, God shows us our hearts by withholding what we want. I have a close friend who wanted babies every bit as much as I did. Her one and only goal in life was to be a stay-at-home mom, and her world was thrown into chaos when she was told she would never conceive a child. We had the same idolatry, but God worked in our hearts in different ways. By withholding what she wanted, God showed her the anger she was capable of feeling toward him. She learned that she could be bitter, resentful, jealous, and hateful toward women who seemed to pop out babies easily when she could not. She learned how much of her identity had been invested in a dream and how she was tempted to worship the idol of motherhood in many ways.

I learned the same lessons. With tremendous shame and grief, I learned that I was capable of hating those small, precious children when they interrupted my agenda or revealed my sin. I was also capable of tremendous bitterness, resentment, jealousy, and anger when overwhelmed by the demands of my little walking, breathing, tantrum-throwing sinners. We all sin in familiar ways, but there are a multitude of pathways along which God will take us to show us our hearts gradually and bring us to humility and repentance. In his kindness God measures out varying doses of wilderness and oasis, crushing difficulty and healing peace, until we come to believe, by experience, that indeed above all things our hearts truly are deceitful and desperately wicked.

In the wilderness experiences of life we learn that, as Jack Miller used to say, we are more sinful than we ever imagined and more loved than we ever dared to hope. Our sin may surprise us immensely, but it is never a surprise to God. Sin blinds us to ourselves, causing us to believe we are much better than we are and much better than others are. God lovingly opens our eyes so that we can repent and can marvel that Christ willingly left the glories of heaven to suffer and die for profound sinners like us. When we are in the wilderness, the obedience of Christ on our behalf can become a cherished doctrine. The more deeply we see our sin, the more grateful we become for the perfect obedience of our Savior credited to us.

WHAT IS GOD UP TO?

What is the Lord up to in our wilderness experiences? John Newton saw them as characteristic of the maturing phase of the Christian life. During this period God moves us forward, using both inner and outer conflict to help us see the reality of our inward sin. Now that our faith has grown stronger and we have more experience of God's kindness and nurturing care, God begins to walk us through experiences with our hearts that would have undone us at an earlier stage of growth.

God is too kind to show us all our sin at one time or at a time when we are too immature to bear the sight. Instead, in this maturing phase of growth, he measures out careful doses of clarity as he leads us to a greater understanding of what Christ has done for us. To be sure, the maturing believer has had many experiences of sin in his life prior to this. The big difference at this point in time is insight. At an earlier time he might simply have stomped away in anger or laid all the blame at the feet of his circumstances. Now, however, the Holy Spirit is at work in the context of specific sins, opening his blind eyes to see a glimpse of his soul. It is not a pretty sight.

In all of this, Newton maintained an absolute certainty of God's specific sovereignty in the life of each believer. By bringing us into situations where we sin and reveal the truth about our hearts, our loving heavenly Father teaches us. He isn't testing us to find out what we will do. He knows all things, and he knows our hearts better than we do. God leads us into these situations because he wants *us* to learn something about ourselves. Oh, I have known for years that in general I am a sinner, but I am prone to living in a foggy blindness to myself day after day. The Bible tells me that above all things I have a heart that is deceitful and desperately wicked (Jer. 17:9), so I shouldn't be surprised to discover the specific ways that I sin—time and time again.

The Bible also tells me that, left to myself, I am prone to exchange the truth of God for lies, to suppress the truth about God and myself, and to live in willful blindness to my own sin while I worship created things instead of the Creator (Rom. 1:18–25). Through these situations of conflict and failure, God reveals that reality clearly to us and to others, to draw us into deeper dependence on him for daily grace and strength.

A PUZZLING DILEMMA

At this point Newton's views of God's purposes—and of Christian maturity—begin to depart from those held by many evangelical Christians today. What is God's goal for us as we mature in faith? Is it simply that we actually sin less and less, or rather that we see our sin more and more? If his goal is that we see more and more sin, then he is ordaining to leave and tolerate a great deal of sin in us for his higher purpose. Since God hates sin and teaches his children to hate it also, it might seem logical to us that he would free us from the power of indwelling sin at the same time that he freed us from the power of sin to send us to hell. If he had done that, then we would have become completely perfect at the time of salvation and been left to experience the rest of our lives here on earth in a sinless state. His will, however, has appointed otherwise.

Instead, at the moment of conversion he frees us from the spiritual power that our sin had to condemn us, but he leaves us with a sinful nature that will wage war against our new nature for the remainder of our lives. When he takes us to be with him in heaven, sin's power over us will fully and finally be broken. In the meantime, it will often win. Many believers naively underestimate the power of this inner sinful man that is left to do battle with our new nature.

One of our problems today is that, while we rightly notice that God hates sin, we often fail to see in Scripture God's sovereignty over it and his willingness to tolerate a great deal of it from the Garden of Eden onward in order to accomplish his holy goals.[7] It may come as a shocking thought that God ordains sin! We know from Scripture that he never tempts anyone to evil and cannot be tempted by it himself (James 1:13). However, it is equally clear that a God who could stop sin and chooses not to, but chooses instead to use it for his own ends, has clearly willed it without ever causing it. We will discuss this idea in more depth later. For now, let's just notice that it matters very much what you believe about God and sin.

If you think that because God hates sin he must be frustrated and disappointed in you every time you sin, then you will be discouraged in this phase of Christian growth. Perhaps that's where you are as you read this. You expect much better of yourself as a Christian, and you're sure that God does too. Yet you find yourself sinning a great deal even when you try your hardest not to. Indeed, this is where I connect with most believers in my counseling experience. They are confused and undone by the ongoing struggle and their lack of progress in holiness, and they fear that in consequence God will give up on them.

However, if you believe that God is completely sovereign over your sin and is always using it for your own good to teach you more about yourself and more of his grace, then you are free to hate your sin but love what God is doing through it. This does not lead to discouragement, fear, anxiety, and depression. On the contrary, it leads to peace, joy, and greater confidence in the work of the Holy Spirit living in you. As Newton observed, "Every day draws forth some new corruption which before was little observed, or at least discovers it in a stronger light than before. Thus by degrees they are weaned from leaning to any supposed wisdom, power, or goodness in themselves; they feel the truth of our Lord's words, 'Without me you can do nothing.'"[8]

If the goal of sanctification is actually growing in humility and greater dependence on Christ, then the Holy Spirit is doing an excellent job. Through his ongoing struggles with indwelling sin, the maturing believer will spend many years learning that he is more sinful than he ever imagined, in order to discover that he is indeed far more loved than he ever dared to hope.

FOR FURTHER REFLECTION

1. What kinds of things cause you to doubt your salvation? What would persuade you that God is always for you and will never abandon you?

2. What do you think growth in faith should look like? How is the maturing believer different from the baby Christian?

3. What is the role of the Holy Spirit in your growth?

4. Has there been a time in your life when God withheld from you something you desperately wanted and prayed

for? Have there been times when he has answered your prayers abundantly? What did you learn about him and about yourself?

5. What is the present wilderness of your life? How is your heart responding to God like Israel did in the wilderness? How is God using his school of experience to teach you more about your heart and more about his love?

6. Do you believe that God is sovereign over all of your sin? Why or why not?

CHAPTER FOUR

grown-ups in faith

His great business is to behold the glory of God in Christ;
and by beholding, he is changed. —John Newton[1]

The mature Christian is distinguished from the baby and from the growing child in several noticeable ways. However, Newton begins his discussion on this subject by noticing several ways in which the adult believer is similar to the infant. He is still in the same state of absolute dependence upon Christ as the infant was. He is just as incapable of performing spiritual acts or resisting temptation on his own as he was on the day he was saved. It is still true that without Christ he can do nothing, and left to himself he will do nothing but sin.

However, in some ways, the mature Christian is much stronger than he was before because he has a deeper and more constant sense of his own weakness. God has been teaching him this lesson for a long time, and by the loving grace of his heavenly Father, his suffering has not been in vain! His heart has deceived him so many times that he has learned to distrust himself more readily and make provision for his own weakness. Because the grown-up Christian knows that he falls easily, he avoids situations that are difficult and tempt him to sin. He is wary of Satan's tricks and asks for help quickly from other Christians and from God. He is not too proud to admit his failures, confessing and repenting rapidly when he falls. He is also not so easily disappointed in himself and others because his expectations have changed and he now understands that both he and his fellow believers are very weak and can do nothing without Christ. Ironically, in all his weakness he is growing steadier in Christ, for he has learned to run to the throne of grace quickly in his times of need. As the Lord told the apostle Paul, "My grace is sufficient for you, for my power is made perfect in weakness" (2 Cor. 12:9). He is stronger in Christ and not in himself.

The superiority of the grown-up in Christ to his younger counterparts lies chiefly in the fact that the Lord has blessed his going to church, praying, listening to biblical preaching, and receiving the Lord's Supper and has given him a clearer view of the greatness and majesty of Christ. He knows his own heart well, and he has also come to see the love of his Savior in deeper and richer ways. His theological knowledge is more solid, his mind more fixed, and his thoughts more focused on the person and work of his Redeemer. He sees the excellence of the Lord Jesus Christ, both in his person and in the ministry that he carries out for the church as prophet, priest, and king. He grasps the great mysteries of redeeming love and cherishes the One who took on human weakness in order to atone for his sin. He marvels at the stability, unity, beauty, and certainty of the Scriptures and frequently meditates on the height, breadth, depth, and length of the love of God in Christ for him. In fact, his greatest joy is to behold the glory of God in Christ, and as he gazes at his Savior he is gradually changed into the likeness of the one he adores. As he delights in Christ more and more, he manifests more consistently the fruits of righteousness by the power of the Holy Spirit, to the glory and praise of God.

The mature Christian's thoughts about God are no longer merely lofty theological ideas or empty philosophical speculations. Instead, the doctrines that he cherishes so much have now traveled from his head to his heart and have begun to change him from the inside out in three primary ways. He is becoming someone who is humble, someone who is spiritual, and someone who is passionate for the glory of God to be displayed in all things.

HUMILITY

The baby Christian and the maturing believer know that they ought to be humble. They begin to see how pride invades every crevice of their thoughts, and they start trying to be humble, yet they often fail. The grown-up in Christ, however, *is* truly humble. He habitually looks back on the way God has faithfully led him and can see the innumerable times that God has given him good in return for his evil. He makes a practice of building monuments in his heart, both to God's goodness and to his own perversity. In the Old Testament, Israel raised up a memorial stone to the Lord's faithfulness after a battle at a place they called "Ebenezer" (1 Sam. 7:12). In the same way, Newton suggests, as the godly Christian recalls each time he has sinned greatly against the Lord, particularly in a high-handed way, he should construct an "Ebenezer"—a mental memorial to his own weakness and sinfulness.[2] But the mature believer never stops at the reminder of his own sinfulness to mourn and despair. He is sorrowful over his sin, yet goes on to build in his mind yet another, even greater, monument to the faithfulness of God in spite of his sin.

In this way, like the apostle Paul, the mature Christian goes through life always sorrowing, but always rejoicing (2 Cor. 6:10). He grieves over his sin because he knows that God hates sin, and he sees how his sin harms himself and others. However, he rejoices even more than he grieves, for he also sees God's patience and faithfulness to him in the context of his continued disobedience. He understands that God is sovereign over his sin and will even use it to shape and strengthen the people in his life against whom he habitually sins. He marvels at the love that refuses to let him go and celebrates God's power to use even his sin to lead him to a deeper understanding of God's grace. He mourns his own lack of righteousness but delights and frolics in the perfect righteousness given to him by Christ. Newton compared these actions to a tune in which the bass line is self-humiliation over sin and the melody is rejoicing over God's faithfulness. When played together, the music is breathtaking.[3]

Although his outward acts may be more moral, the grown-up Christian often actually feels more sinful than he did in his earlier years, for he sees his sin with more clarity, accuracy, and frequency. He has discovered that his obedience tempts him to sin as much as his sinful desires and over-desires do. He has learned the insidious nature of his own pride, and though he can't escape it, he truly hates the internal voice of self-glorification that narrates the story of his life when he is at his most obedient. His days are therefore filled with the dialogue of prayer because he has learned his desperate need for God and runs often to the Lord for help.

He plans for his own weakness by anticipating areas of struggle and doing all that is in his power to protect himself against temptation. He does not try to outsmart Satan. He knows that Satan is an expert in his field and far beyond him in strength and cunning. So he casts himself repeatedly on the Lord's grace and pleads for mercy in his time of need. He has learned to live a life of continual repentance before God, confessing his sins freely and often, and living at the foot of the cross where he is bathed in forgiveness and hope every day, even as often as he sins.

Another aspect of the mature believer's humility is his quickness to submit to the will of God. He has been wrong so many times before that he no longer dares to presume upon the will of God, but instead looks eagerly for what God will do in each situation. He has predicted what the answers to his prayers ought to be, only to find that God's answer was a complete surprise and far superior to anything he could have imagined. He has anticipated that some people were headed for a sad ending, only to find that God's grace to preserve and transform them far surpassed his expectations. He has predicted a glorious future for others, only to see them humbled and chastened under the mighty hand of God. He has fought hard to impose his own will on others, only to encounter disaster when God allowed him to succeed. He has watched God use great suffering to bless the lives of some of his friends, while he has watched prosperity ruin others. Therefore his knowledge of himself and of the majesty of God causes him to shrink into the dust. He truly believes that God is wiser and more loving than he could ever be, and so he looks for God's hand of loving care in every trial, whether his own or those of people around him.

TENDERNESS

The mature believer also has a tender spirit toward his fellow Christians. He must at times evaluate their conduct, but the knowledge he has of the weakness and sinfulness of his own heart causes him to be gentle and to make every possible allowance for the weakness of others. In other words, he is most aware of the beam in his own eye as he gazes on the splinters in the eyes of his brothers and sisters (Matt. 7:3-4). He knows that all human beings are weak and made of dust, just like him. He understands that we live in a world full of temptation that constantly beckons us to indulge, taste, sample, and satiate ourselves with sinful delights. He understands that there is a powerful spiritual enemy who is an expert at temptation, and he has often experienced the torment of Satan's rage. He also knows his own record of wrongs, and this qualifies him to admonish and restore others with a spirit of gentleness and meekness.

In this area, Newton observes, the baby Christian is often prone to sin. The zeal of his enthusiastic feelings, not yet balanced by a true sense of his own imperfections, leads him to rebuke others with a prideful and censorious spirit. But the grown-up Christian can bear with the youngster patiently because he has been there himself and will not expect fruit to be ripe before its due season.

In fact, Newton compares the young believer to a green nectarine.[4] It would be ludicrous to go to a nectarine tree in the early summer and strip it of its fruit simply because it is all still green. We know that with just a few more days of rain, and a few more days of sun, this fruit will ripen to delicious sweetness. So it is with the baby Christian. His misguided zeal may be annoying and even harmful to himself and others right now, but the Lord knows those who are his and he will not let them go. They can't escape his pruning and shaping and will inevitably reach maturity—if not in this life, then surely in the next.

This is one reason I know that I am not a mature Christian. Each time I try to congratulate myself on how I have grown, forgetting completely that all growth is God's work, he sends a baby Christian across my path and I get really annoyed. Two months ago a young woman who was filled with the joy and delight of reading the Scriptures stayed with us. She loved reading the Bible, and she loved telling everyone how much she enjoyed it and what great quiet times she had. Did I celebrate with her and for her, rejoicing that God had given her such a sweet gift at this point in her walk with him? No! I got irritated because I find it difficult to read God's Word and I rarely want to do it at all. I have such a weak appetite for Scripture that I have to schedule things into my week to force me to read it, or I would never pick it up. So I teach Bible studies and I put together worship services, and as I do these things I am always blessed by Scripture and often moved to tears. But I still find it hard to want to read the Bible.

As a result, I wanted to pop this infant's bubble and give her a piece of my mind. But then, irony of ironies, one of my sons was reflecting on this young woman's zeal and mentioned how sweet and wonderful it was that this young lady delighted in reading the Bible. This was adding insult to injury! I considered myself much more spiritually mature than my son, and yet here he was behaving with far more adult behavior than I was! Although I might classify myself as a maturing believer, and have been for a few years, the ease with which I revert to this type of judgmental legalism is sobering. I am as much in need of God's grace to stand in obedience today as I was at the age of 6, when I first accepted Christ. God is so kind and merciful; whenever I begin to steal the glory for his work once again, he lets me fall, just to remind me how weak and broken I really am.

SPIRITUALITY

Another characteristic of mature Christians is that they understand the danger of being too attached to worldly pleasures. They know that with our human nature we "cleave to the dust in defiance to the dictates of our better judgment,"[5] and are drawn toward the improper and excessive use of God's good gifts. The grown-up believer is not perfect in this respect, but worldly things will not be his prevailing choice. Newton recognized that we often see younger Christians clogged and entangled in many worldly indulgences. He observed that God seldom gives his children significant victory over this evil until he has shown them just how deeply rooted it is in their hearts. We see this principle at work often in our churches today. We call it addiction.

I counsel many earnest young Christians who are struggling with addiction. The substances to which they are addicted vary a great deal, but the heart desires that drive these addictions are the same. They are addicted to food, health, drugs, porn, good grades, exercise, thinness, sex, work, alcohol, and even parental approval. The list of possibilities is as long as the list of good things that God has created—things we use to try to make ourselves feel good. When a Christian struggles with a besetting sin in the form of an addiction, it is tempting to try to change the behavior while missing the bigger picture of what God is doing in the heart. Most addictions feel fun for a while, but eventually they lose their attraction and leave strugglers hating the behavior and trying everything they can think of to stop.

However, God may change their will long before he actually gives them the spiritual fruit of self-control in that specific area, and Newton tells us that God has a profound purpose in this. When God changes the will and gives someone a great desire for obedience but not the strength to withstand temptation, he is putting his child in a painful and difficult position. Yet he does this in love and not with judgment or punishment in mind. He is humbling this child in a powerful way and crushing the child's self-reliance. This can feel like a curse, when it is actually a great gift.

Newton states that most mature Christians have struggled with besetting sin in some form or other, for God rarely sets his children free from it before he has used it to teach them valuable lessons. Humans are toxically self-reliant and prideful creatures who tend to believe they can do anything they set their minds to. In their early days of indulgence most addicts believe that they can stop the behavior whenever they choose. Before they know it, however, they are habitually drawn to the relief that their addiction offers and are unable to walk away. In his kindness God shows his people how weak they are by turning them over to the object of their desire and letting them flounder in it, sometimes for a long period of time. God is a good father who lets his children fall in order to protect them in the end.

STEPPING AWAY

Our older daughter, Hannah, was born with a gleam in her eye. She was a determined child right from the start, and she chose to wage war on the battleground of the staircase. She was our only early walker, and she was excited about moving from the time she first got up on her hands and knees. She was also observant and noticed that her two older brothers went up and down the staircase on their feet. She wanted to be just like them. As we had done with her older siblings, we taught her to scoot down the stairs on her bottom. She was tiny and her balance was still shaky and weak, and we knew that going downstairs facing forward and on her feet was risky business. She couldn't even reach the handrail! Yet every time we turned our backs for a minute, there she was, crawling up the stairs and then standing up and turning around to come down in her favorite upright position. So we put up baby gates and watched her closely, but this didn't stop her from seeking every unguarded moment to try again, especially at other people's homes.

So we decided to let her fall down. We didn't let her climb high or fall far, and we made sure her pathway for falling was safe, but we stopped rescuing her. Sure enough, our little acrobat headed right for the stairs once again. This time, when she'd gone up a few steps and turned to do her little trick, we didn't react. We warned her, but the sparkle of mischief in her eyes betrayed her determination to beat us at this game. That is, until she fell down several times! It didn't take long for her to figure out that falling down is scary and it hurts a lot! Then she stopped trying until she was much stronger and steadier. In the end she was safer than when we had watched her like hawks because she had become convinced of something by experience. This experience of pain protected her whether we were nearby or far away, at home or somewhere else. Good parents sometimes let

71

their children suffer painful experiences in order to teach them important, even life-saving lessons.

God is a far better father than any human could ever be. Like the father in the parable of the prodigal son, he lets his children go, sometimes for long periods of time. He waits patiently for them to exhaust themselves with sin and reach the end of their rope, and then he lovingly welcomes them back as they trudge homeward. They need to learn where true love and joy are found, and they need to learn their weakness and inability to change themselves before they will ever cherish his power and salvation.

As a result of their many falls, grown-up Christians are wary and on guard. They know the dangerous deception of worldly pleasures and their own tendency to become trapped by them. They are fully aware of the evils of attachment to them, are more watchful against them, and are thus more often delivered from them. They know that they are weak, and therefore they are more careful not to put themselves in situations that are dangerous and tempting.

IN SICKNESS AND IN HEALTH . . . TILL DEATH DO US PART

Mature Christians are also able to fix their eyes on Christ, even when the world is caving in all around them (Ps. 46:1–3). Their joy is not based on their circumstances but is founded on what Christ has done for them. In consequence, they do not doubt God's love when suffering and hardship come, and they don't drift away and think they don't need God if he gives them riches and prosperity. They hold their possessions and wealth lightly, knowing that the God who has given them may one day take them away as well. They do not believe that God owes them an easy life, but instead they willingly accept all of their circumstances as coming from the Father's loving hand. They are therefore steady, firm, and not easily shaken by the disasters of life. They grieve when death and sorrow come, but they grieve with a strong assurance of faith and a steady hope in the promises of God.

Mature believers tend to view death differently from their younger siblings in Christ as well. Newton notes that we are earthly people, and we aren't inclined to spend a great deal of time thinking about heaven. The grown-up Christian is much different. He longs for heaven and would easily choose heaven over earth if he didn't have other people to think about. He longs to depart and be with Christ, just as the apostle Paul did (Phil. 1:23), but the selfish aspects of this longing are not lost on him. He knows there are many people left to love and serve here, so he dreams of heaven but keeps his feet firmly rooted in the ministry that God has given him to do on earth. He is heavenly minded and full of earthly good.

The mature Christian can't wait to see his Savior face to face and to fall at his feet. He is tired of his sinful self and eager to shed his body of death and walk into eternity.[6] From time to time, when God is pleased to give him a glimpse of heaven, his heart explodes with gratitude and joy all at once. This may happen as he worships, or reads Scripture, or listens to music, or for no apparent reason at all. Suddenly he is transported and finds his heart blazing with love for God and an almost unbearable sense of God's love for him.

He does not demand such moments, or prolong them, or go in search of them. But he knows they are a token of what is to come, a foretaste of the day when he will fall on his knees before the Lamb of God, completely lost in wonder, love, and praise. Then he will be transformed in an instant and will see the object of his longing with joy and clarity. Then he will touch the scarred hands held out to him in welcome, and faith will become sight once and for all. These glimpses of heaven fuel his heart with energy and determination, for they remind him that Jesus Christ will come again to claim him and take him home. Although very few of us will reach great spiritual maturity in this life, there is no need to despair. By God's rich and loving grace we will all get there in the end: we will instantly be transformed into his image because we will see him with our own eyes!

FOR FURTHER REFLECTION

1. How has God been changing you as you walk through life with him? What tools have been powerful implements of growth in your life lately?

2. What spiritual truths are transforming the growing Christian? Are those same truths having an impact in your life right now, or do they seem distant and powerless? Why?

3. Are you more humble than you were as a younger believer? In what ways do you see pride still affecting your relationship with God? With others?

4. What monuments to your own perversity mark the pathway of your life? Do you think of them often or do you want to forget them and hide them from others? What monuments to God's faithfulness have you raised up in your life? Do you dwell on them often? Why do your thoughts go where they do most often?

5. What impact would it have on you if you dwelt on the mountain of your sin but didn't look at the higher mountain of God's faithfulness to you in spite of it? What impact might it have if you only saw God's goodness and never remembered your sin? What good fruit comes from dwelling often on these truths together?

6. Newton describes our sin as the bass line of the music of our lives, and the gospel as the sweet melody. What is the song of your life like? Is it heavy on the bass and light on the melody? Is it all melody and no harmony? Why?

CHAPTER FIVE

the disney delusion

Sir, we hear much in the present day of the
dignity of human nature. —John Newton[1]

Most of us are experts at hiding our weakness. It's no fun to be weak, and we work hard to deny our weakness to ourselves and to hide it from others. This is an enormous problem for us as Christians, and it causes chaos and pain in our own and others' lives.

We are profoundly confused about what God expects of us and what we are actually capable of achieving in this life. This confusion, though tragic, is not surprising. We Americans in particular live in a culture that teaches us from our youngest days in preschool that simply believing something makes it true, and that no one can stop us from reaching our dreams. If Newton was concerned in his day that there was so much talk about the dignity of human nature that the fallenness of our natural condition was becoming obscured, what would he say about our day? Rags-to-riches stories are heralded by the media as proof that anyone can be anything they want to be. This results in foolish hopes and aspirations being nurtured far longer than the harsh realities of this world would condone.

I love Walt Disney, but I am also concerned about the powerful impact of his movies. This fact hit home a few years ago when our church music director decided to host a Disney-themed coffeehouse at our home, just for fun. Magic ruled that night as our traditionally furnished home was transformed into a classy, moodily lit space, sparkling with candlelight and infused with the aroma of coffee and frothy milk.

We had always enjoyed Disney movies with our children when they were small, though we were also eager and diligent to critique them biblically and help our kids watch them from a Christian worldview. My oldest son tells me that to this day he cannot watch a Disney movie without hearing my voice in his head: *Now Jamie, do you agree with Jiminy Cricket? Do you think the Bible teaches us to let our conscience be our guide?* I'm sure we wearied our children with our earnest attempts to teach them to enjoy the world God gave them with wisdom and discernment. Nevertheless, the tales of Pinocchio, Sleeping Beauty, Cinderella, Mowgli, and Mary Poppins nourished the God-given, image-bearing gifts of imagination and creativity in our children.

These movies, with their idealistic and humanistic themed messages about fulfilling potential, hovered in the background of my children's lives, and I sometimes worried about the expectations they were shaping in the hearts of impressionable little people. My daughters played princess often and visibly longed for palaces, jewels, and, of course, the handsome prince. My daughter Hannah was young when she responded to discipline by informing me that I was not her real mother. She was actually a princess, and someday I would be sorry when her real parents claimed her and she put me in prison for the rest of my life. Of course, you may say, this is a common enough fantasy—one in which we have all engaged at some time. However, on the night of the Disney coffeehouse, I began to suspect that the realm of

fantasy had dangerously merged with reality for a whole genera-
tion of young people.

THE POWER OF MAKE-BELIEVE

Our house was packed with enthusiastic college students
dressed up as Disney characters. The music was captivating and
the performances remarkable, but what struck me that night
was the commitment of these young people to the stories and
songs of the fairy tales. These students didn't just *watch* Disney
movies from time to time in their formative years, they *grew up
on* Disney. They knew every word to every song, and some of
them were able to repeat entire scripts with complete dialogues!
They were passionate about the characters and enchanted by the
antics and actions of the heroes and heroines, and they deeply
identified with the beloved characters of their dreamy tales.
These smart, prosperous, high-achieving young adults suffered
from a serious devotion to the world of make-believe, and that
night I began to wonder just how much Disney-ism had crept
into their spiritual lives as well. The notion that you can be all
that you want to be if you only believe can be harmful enough
in the kindergartens of this world, but when transported into
the church, it is deadly.

Disney beckons us to identify with the oppressed characters
of lore whose inner greatness is veiled for a while, but is gloriously
revealed through overcoming adversity. In our self-centered little
worlds, we turn inward to imagine ourselves as stronger, smarter,
and far better looking than we actually are. What a delicious
thing it is to sink into the realm of fantasy and pretend that we
are what we are not, or that we are not what we actually are. Of
course, most of us realize sooner or later that fantasy doesn't
get us a long way in real life, and we go about the tough business
of accepting reality and working with what we have actually
been given. Instead of the astronauts, firemen, ballet dancers,

and princesses we dreamed of becoming in kindergarten, most of us become engineers, plumbers, teachers, and accountants.

CHRISTIAN MAKE-BELIEVE

However, when the Disney message is loudly proclaimed from the pulpits of well-meaning, Bible-believing churches, it is devastating to God's people. It tells us that if we just have enough faith, we can do or be anything we want to. We may not succumb to the crassest form of this belief that infects many churches, the form that teaches that our faith can make us healthy and wealthy. Yet we often buy into a more subtle form of the same malady. We really believe that if we have enough faith and try really, really hard that we can stop sinning and be just like Jesus. We are taught that it is within our power to allow or inhibit God's work of sanctification in our lives, so that our progress in personal holiness is up to us. If we try harder and cooperate with God, we can succeed and achieve virtual perfection, becoming spiritual princes and princesses. If we choose not to be fully committed to God, however, he is powerless to change us and can't possibly bless us as he longs to do.

That view ascribes far too much power to people who are actually very weak and full of sin. God planned it this way, remember? He could have made us strong or even perfect the moment he saved each of us, but he didn't. Instead, he sent his Spirit to take up residence in people who are still bound to sinful flesh and full of remaining sin. As God calls us to obedience, *he* remembers that we are only dust, but we keep forgetting. We think that with a wish, a sprinkle of fairy dust, a great quiet time, and some prayer, we can all be spiritual heroes and do great things for God. We couldn't be more wrong, and as a result, we are devastated when reality crashes into fantasy day after grueling day.

Every week I counsel young people from solid Christian homes who are undone by their sin. As parents, we are sometimes more invested in protecting our children from the sinful influences of this world than we are in preparing them for the deep sinfulness of their own hearts. We think that if we can just keep them from sinning too much while they are young and vulnerable, then they won't struggle with sin so much as adults. Of course, good parents don't allow their kids to sin much. They discipline, teach, restrain, and intervene. Yet these actions alone don't prepare young people well for the reality of the powerful temptations they will face when Mom and Dad aren't around. Simply building a fence between a child and temptation is not the same thing as preparing him to face life.

If we are honest and wise we will remind our children that they are depraved little sinners right from the start, that being naughty is easy and natural for kids and moms and dads, and that obeying is far beyond our ability. If we deny that reality by acting terribly surprised each time they sin and saying "How could you do that?" it is not surprising that our children become confused. No wonder college campuses are overflowing with young Christian men and women who know that they are sinners in some global and lofty way, but who fall apart and are shattered with anxiety and depression when they fall into specific sin. They are shocked by their own desires and behavior, and they find themselves turning to harmful addictions or to the manic pursuit of Christian disciplines in order to pacify their desperate feelings of failure and inadequacy.

THE WEAKNESS OF STRENGTH AND
THE STRENGTH OF WEAKNESS

I think we are afraid to believe that we are weak (or to help our kids know that they are weak) because we fear that admitting weakness is the same thing as condoning sin. However, in my experience, admitting our weakness actually leads to less sin. But first we must understand what the Bible says about weakness and strength. In the Bible, the strongest people are those who know their own weakness while the weakest people are those who are most impressed by their own strength. The history of God's own people bears witness to this fact.

Nowhere in the Old Testament do we see Israel as an obedient and righteous people, merrily keeping God's law. On the contrary, right after God gave his people the law on Mount Sinai, complete with lightning, thunder, and scary sound effects, the people broke the covenant they had made with God by crafting a golden calf (Ex. 32). From the outset, God's people engaged in a consistent pattern of sin that would end up in their exile from the land God had given them. The story of God's chosen people is one exhausting, demoralizing, and discouraging tale of disobedience, sin, rebellion, and hatred for God. It is also a dazzling tale of love and rescue, as God preserves a remnant for himself in spite of all of their sin and disobedience.

Even the biggest heroes of the Old Testament were frequently ensnared in idolatrous sin and were in great need of the Savior that their best moments foreshadowed. Abraham lied about Sarah being his wife (Gen. 12) and allowed himself to be talked into taking a concubine (Gen. 16), David was an adulterer and a murderer (2 Sam. 11), while Solomon multiplied horses and chariots as well as acquiring many foreign wives for whom he ended up building idolatrous temples (1 Kings 11). As a result of all of this weakness and sin, however, the Old Testament is also one breathtaking tale after another of God's patience, longsuffering, kindness, and love toward those he has chosen to redeem. Without the vastness of the people's sin there would have been no context to display the greatness of God's grace.

It is no different when we come to the New Testament. The apostles were hardly shining examples of holy living. James and John wanted to call down fire from heaven on a Samaritan village (Luke 9:54). Peter wanted to stop Jesus from going to the cross

(Matt. 16:21–23) and was afraid of standing up to the Judaizers in Galatia (Gal. 2:12). Paul and Barnabas couldn't agree on whether to give John Mark a second chance after he let them down on his first missions trip (Acts 15:37–39). Paul even calls himself the chief of sinners (see 1 Tim. 1:15) and explains his inability to obey God in great detail in Romans 7 and Galatians 5. Yet Jesus reserved his most caustic rebukes for the Pharisees, the people who were far more committed to performing acts of righteousness than any of us are (Luke 11:42–44).

Given this context, it is not surprising to read Paul's teaching in the New Testament about weakness. If the story of redemption is about us gradually becoming more and more sinless, then Paul's boasting in his weakness makes no sense whatsoever (2 Cor. 11:30). But, if the story of redemption is about Jesus and his righteousness, then our continuing weakness actually shines the spotlight on Jesus all the more brightly. Paul's description of himself as chief of sinners (see 1 Tim. 1:15–16) is not some charming attempt at humility and self-abasement; it is the absolute, glorious truth. We are all frail and fragile children who sin a great deal in our disobedience, but who also manage to sin a great deal in our best obedience as well. Discovering this truth and growing to love it can be one of the most powerful and joyful motivations for change that God ever invented, but it seems that few Christians today ever get there. They have such a hard time giving up their great expectations for themselves and others, and they are left spinning aimlessly in cycles of fear and shame as they try desperately to impose those expectations on the recalcitrant world around them.

It may be beneficial to stop for a moment and examine your own expectations of yourself and those around you. What do you think God expects of you as a redeemed sinner? Are those expectations shaped by the whole counsel of God's Word? Do you tend to dwell on those passages of Scripture that call you to try hard to obey and forget the passages which remind you that God is patient with his weak children? Are your expectations shaped by demanding parents whose approval of you depended on your performance? Have you been influenced by preaching that is overly hopeful about change and laced with ideas of perfectionism? Does Disney have such a grip on your mind and heart that you can't let go of your Christian dreams of pleasing God by means of your own goodness?

If you are a parent, are you helping your children to understand their sinful hearts and turn to Christ in their failure, or are you afraid that compassion for their sinful state will make them sin more? Do you show understanding and grace to your friends when they sin against you and others, or are you cold and inflexible in your condemnation of them?

A CASE FOR JOY

You will never be able to find steady joy in this life until you understand, submit to, and even embrace the fact that you are weak and sinful. Does that sound shocking? The truth is that only weak and sinful people really need a redeemer. Paul boasted in his weakness and gloried in the fact that he was the chief of sinners because he believed beyond all doubt that God had ordained that weakness and brokenness for Paul's personal benefit as well as for God's own glory. You may think that you would actually bring God more glory through your strength and obedience than through failure. Yet the Sovereign Lord of the Universe appears to disagree with you. God is supremely interested in the glory of his Son and delights in the way that glory is revealed in his love for wicked people who continue to need his grace and mercy day after day. Accepting your weakness opens up new avenues of delight in your Savior—new corridors of worship and awe as you contemplate all that he is to you as you really are, inside and out.

Can we even move beyond accepting our weakness to enjoying it? What could there possibly be to enjoy about your own weakness? Let me answer that question with a story. I spent decades despising my weakness, and the fruit of this hatred in my life was not pretty. For fifteen long and tortuous years I was very fat. By "very fat," I mean clinically obese: 140 pounds overweight. I would have done anything, and indeed tried everything, to overcome this sinful obsession with food. I was a faithful and sometimes highly successful member of Weight Watchers. I attended every Christian weight loss group I could find, read every book, prayed, journaled, fasted, and paid expensive counselors to help me overcome this problem.

By God's grace, I knew my overeating was sin, and I called it sin—that made it so much more painful than if I could have pretended it was my glands. It also made it so much more shameful and embarrassing: just one quick glance would let everyone know this particular pastor's wife was a huge, gigantic, jiggling sinful mess. Every day I woke up with a determination to change, and every day I ate compulsively in response to any and every emotion. I ate when I was sad, angry, bored, fearful, and anxious. I also ate when I was happy, excited, hopeful, and delighted by my life. I was in deep trouble as I compulsively ate my way through each and every day in spite of my hatred for this sin and desperate desire to change. More than anything, I hated the fact that I couldn't just decide to change when I wanted to. Is there anything in the world more humiliating than that?

With my great pride, I was determined that I would beat this thing. God simply didn't let me do it. I knew some great theology at the time and understood that if he wanted me to change, I would. However, my anger toward him only increased when I thought about the fact that he could restrain my sin but he chose not to. What a mean and vexing God he must be to play with my emotions this way. After all, what I wanted was a *good* thing, even a *great* thing. I wanted the fruit of the Spirit—at least some of it! I wanted self-control, but in all honesty, I wanted it for sinful reasons. Actually, what I wanted was the "fruit of Barb" and not the fruit of the Spirit. I wanted to choose to change, and I wanted the credit when change would come. Of course, I would tell everyone that God gave me the strength to stop eating, but even my fantasy life was permeated with the praise and respect I would get when I lost all that weight and kept it off forever. In my frustration and foulness, I was blind to all the very real fruit of the very real and powerful Spirit of the living God, which he was working in me *through* this very sin.

Without even knowing it, I was becoming more compassionate toward others. Instead of judging and rejecting them for their problems, I was beginning to think new thoughts like, *Well, they may be weak in an area where I am strong, but look at me! If I can't just get over my struggle with food, maybe they are experiencing the same thing and they can't just change.* Critique and censure began to give way to empathy and sorrow: *I'll bet it is really hard and embarrassing to struggle with that. . . . I wonder how I can help and encourage them.* I was becoming more patient with my husband and with my kids. If I was still failing over and over with a simple thing like eating, then I would have to give others the permission to do the same in their areas of weakness. I was becoming more loving toward difficult people and kinder toward awkward people. I was becoming gentler in my dealings with everyone and more willing to commit to love them faithfully over the long haul, even when they didn't change at all. Above all, I was becoming more joyful in Christ and far more peaceful about the fact that he loved me just as I was, sin and all.

As my anger toward God poured out of my heart, I was able to see it clearly and confess it to God and others. Then he kindly granted me repentance. Gluttony was the sin that showed me so many other, less visible sins that had nested in my heart quietly for many years, unseen by me. Yet repentance and change did not come together, as we are so often told they must. God gave me grace to grieve over my sin and hate it long before he granted me the grace to grow in that area.

WHAT GOD WANTS

Joy in Christ is perhaps God's greatest desire for his children. He does not want us to admire ourselves; he wants us to cherish and long for his beloved Son. His goal is to humble us and show us our great need for the ravishing gift he has provided. Sinful weakness is one of the precious tools he uses to help us get there.

As God turned me over to my own abysmal failure year after year, I began to cherish something that had once been only a vague and mysterious notion in my head. I grew up in a Christian home, and I had been diligently taught the doctrine of imputation, but I was taught that it was a one-way deal. My sin was imputed to Christ, and he died in my place. That was a great truth, but it wasn't the whole gospel, and it was somehow devoid of power in my life.

When my husband attended seminary, I began to learn about the doctrine of double imputation—that is, not only was my sin imputed to Christ, but his righteousness was also imputed to me. God not only took away my filthy rags, he also clothed me in the perfect, clean clothes of another. How cool, I thought. What a neat and amazing concept. Yet it remained just a concept until I began to struggle with sin I could not defeat. Oh, the promises I made to God and could not keep! Oh, the complete misery of failure, discouragement, anger, and apathy that I could not break free from. Oh, the hopeless discouragement of addictive cycles that held such a grip on my heart and mind. In those moments of intense despair God began to put a new thought in my mind.

In spite of the good work God was accomplishing in me through this relentless failure, I became fearful and immobilized.

I looked ahead at what life would be like for me, a fat woman growing older, and it was an unpleasant prospect. I was already becoming a spectator in the lives of my children. Moving was becoming more difficult, so that quite often my thin, healthy, and active husband would take the kids on outings, hikes, and visits to the park while I sat at home and ate even more, driven by guilt and sadness over what I was doing to my family and myself. There were many times when I wished to die, and quite a few when I imagined killing myself, utterly persuaded that they would all be so much better off without me.

My disappointment in myself was impossible to bear. How had I come to this? I wasn't abused in any way as I grew up. I was raised in a wonderful, loving, Christian home, and I had absolutely no excuse for my reckless and compulsive behavior. I used food as a medication and a weapon, even though it wasn't very effective as either. I had not yet learned that you don't have to be abused to be messed up; you just have to be human!

At this point in my life I had grown accustomed to listening to sermons while I worked in the kitchen as a form of quiet time. I didn't really enjoy reading the Bible on my own, but I did love listening to gospel-centered sermons by Reformed pastors. I was perpetually exhausted with five little ones to care for and I could invent a million excuses not to have the dreaded "Quiet Time," but sermons were delightful to my soul. As I listened, the theme of Christ's righteousness began to take hold of my heart. I was an out-of-control mess, but Christ ate perfectly for me, and his goodness had been given to me. What an astounding thought this was! Up until this time I had been sure that God loved me better when I kept my dieting promises to him, ate healthily, and lost weight. Now I was beginning to understand that God loved me at every moment just as he loved his Son, Jesus. If my sin was placed on Jesus on the cross, then it was gone forever.

This had to be true of all the sin I had not yet committed, as well as the sins I had already perpetrated against God. If the righteousness of Christ was given to me, fully and completely, then God actually saw me as a perfect eater, with a record of obedience and self-control that I could never achieve. As this doctrine sank deeply into my mind and soul a revolution began to take place. My sin became an opportunity for wondrous celebration of the truth that in Christ I was already justified, sanctified, and glorified, in spite of my wretched and tenacious failure here and now.

I did not give up trying to change, but I began to relax about my persistent inability to change. I already had what I desperately needed: the unshakeable love of the God of the universe and the blissful perfection of his Son who lived life for me and also died for my sin. My heart was pulverized by this truth as I began to rejoice and frolic in the perfection I had in Christ. It seemed like crazy, audacious, and unbelievably generous love that would cause Jesus to go to such extreme lengths for the joy of having me. I knew I wasn't much worth having, and yet for the joy set before him Jesus chose to love me and suffer for me, knowing full well that I would continue to be this weak, this sinful, this idolatrous, and this rebellious, so trapped in the web of my own desires.

This new understanding did not make me want to sin more. On the contrary, it stirred my heart to want to obey. This was the grace a counselor had described to me many years earlier, a grace I couldn't yet imagine or understand. This was grace to stay very weak and to struggle daily with sin, and yet to dance and frolic in the complete certainty of God's love for me. This was to be in Christ, joined to him in his death and his obedience, and to delight in the same love the Father has for him. This was grace to have outrageous joy in the presence of painful failure: grace not just to survive great failure, but to thrive in the face of it. This was amazing, extravagant, and inexplicable grace, where personal pride was lovingly shattered so that all I could possibly do was look to Christ, admire his perfection, and marvel at his love for such a profoundly troubled person.

God is not captivated by our attempts to please him; he is riveted by the obedience of his Son and delighted by the goodness of Jesus Christ. God loves it when we are dazzled by the brilliant glory of his Son as well, and so he will not let us be overly impressed with our own performance for long. In love he shatters the Disney myth, in order to point us to greater joy than we could ever imagine.

In contrast to modern misperceptions, John Newton gives us in his hymn "How Sweet the Name of Jesus Sounds" a more accurate and joyful view of living the Christian life.

> Weak is the effort of my heart
> And cold my warmest thought
> But when I see thee as thou art
> I'll praise thee as I ought.[2]

FOR FURTHER REFLECTION

1. What do you think makes someone a strong Christian? What do you think makes someone a weak Christian? Are you strong? How would you know?

2. When did you last feel great joy in your salvation? Describe what happened, what you were thinking, and how it felt.

3. What great things do you aim to do for Christ? What do you long to be like? In what ways are you tempted to sin while you are being most obedient to God and standing strong?

4. Do you tend to hide your weakness and sinful failure? How might the gospel free you to enjoy it rather than be crushed by it?

5. Why might living under law feel safer and more comfortable than living under grace? What does it mean to be under grace and not under law?

6. How do you feel about yourself when you can't change? How does God feel about you when you can't change?

7. How does your life most glorify God and Jesus? When does it most glorify you?

CHAPTER SIX

saints and sinners

*In defiance of my best judgment and best wishes,
I find something within me which cherishes and cleaves
to those evils from which I ought to start and flee, as I
should if a toad or a serpent was put in my food or in
my bed.* —John Newton[1]

My mind was full of lofty thoughts as I pulled hurriedly into the grocery store parking lot. Ignoring both stop signs and pedestrian walks, I found a spot and squeezed my car carelessly between the painted lines. I was in a hurry, and I hate to be late for anything. I glanced at my list as I headed toward the automatic doors, but higher things were hijacking my full attention. I had spent the morning listening to class lectures on biblical counseling and reading books about human dignity. My soul had been ravished by the gospel in a freshly exciting way, and I was living in a glory cloud. I glanced around as I filled my basket, and wonderful thoughts made their way through my mind. We are image bearers, made to reflect the glory of God; even in our fallen state we bear his signature, the imprint of the divine, corrupted and warped by sin to be sure, but never completely obliterated.

I was enjoying this sweetly altered state of being as I quickly and efficiently found each item I needed. All was going well, and I would be on time after all. As I stood second in line at the checkout, a conversation taking place nearby pulled me out of my reverie. Although the checkout clerk was quick and efficient, groceries were piling up at the end of the conveyor belt, and the bagger seemed to be talking far more than he was bagging. I took a moment to absorb the scene and realized that the bagger, a young man named Edward, seemed to be handicapped in some way. I was now hearing him say the same sentence to the customer in front of me for the third time, "I think it's important to go to the dentist, don't you?" The customer agreed and Edward went on. "I'm afraid of the dentist. I'm afraid he'll be mad at me, so I told the lady that I flossed my teeth when I didn't. I don't want the dentist to be mad at me." The customer nodded his head and began to bag his own groceries. Edward wasn't finished yet. "Do you think I should floss my teeth? I think I should but I don't, and I'm afraid the dentist will be mad at me." As the customer ahead of me collected his bags and disappeared hastily, Edward turned his attention to me. My heart sank as I heard, for a fourth time, "I think it's important to go to the dentist, don't you?"

A series of rapid thoughts flew through my mind. I was in no mood for this; I was in a hurry! I had important things to do and important people to meet. I was about to dismiss this young man with a smile and a nod when I suddenly remembered that Edward, too, was an image bearer. Wounded by life's tragedies and scarred with physical and mental imperfection, he was still made in God's image and worthy of my respect and honor. I knew immediately that God had placed this thought in my mind, because it was not at all characteristic of me.

The Holy Spirit was at work, connecting what I had learned in class to real life in a wonderful way. I took a moment to look at Edward and see him before I smiled and agreed wholeheartedly that it is indeed very important to go to the dentist. I asked him if he had been to the dentist recently, and he told me what he had told the man before me: he had been to the dentist and he had lied. I wondered for a moment how I could enter his world in some way with the few seconds in which our lives would intersect. I agreed with him that dentists can feel like scary people, and that I am also tempted to lie when I am afraid of something. The counselor in me wanted to go for his heart, but I didn't know Edward, and I didn't have time to know him. I lingered for a moment and asked more questions, truly desiring to love him in the small moment we shared. Then it was over, and as I headed out the door I heard him say to the woman behind me, "I think it's important to go to the dentist, don't you?" I went on my way, thanking God for that moment in which I had been rescued from my characteristic brusqueness long enough to bless someone with interest and kind words.

I continued to enjoy wonderful spiritual thoughts as I got into the car and buckled up. As I glanced at the clock and suddenly realized I was going to be late after all, a sense of alarm flooded my body with adrenaline and made my heart pound. I quickly backed out, raced through the parking lot, and pulled into a steady stream of traffic. At least if I hurried I wouldn't be shamefully late.

All was going well until a car pulled out ahead of me and proceeded to drive slowly in front of me for no obvious reason. My agitation grew, and I decided to tailgate him just a little to give him some much-needed encouragement. He did not speed up, and angry thoughts began to fly through my mind: *What is your problem, you idiot? Did you donate your brain to science? There's absolutely no one in front of you, so what kind of a fathead are you?* Then the person behind me, who had decided to tailgate *me* to encourage me to speed up, leaned on his horn and blasted me. The nerve of this guy! I was furious, and I decided I needed to teach him a lesson. I began to drive even more slowly, and I enjoyed his agitation and helplessness as he remained trapped behind me and unable to pass. Streams of vicious thoughts and hateful words passed through the pathways of my brain while I indulged this childish tantrum as long as I could. Finally, the man in front of me turned, and I once again devoted my attention toward getting to my meeting as soon as possible.

It wasn't long before the ridiculous nature of what had just taken place began to dawn on me. In the period of just a few short minutes I had gone from one extreme to another. One moment I had been full of wonderful spiritual thoughts, which had resulted in uncharacteristic actions of love and kindness toward Edward. In the very next moment I had become something else altogether. Surely the men driving in front of and behind me were image bearers as well, and equally worthy of my respect and honor, but there were no good thoughts to rescue me from my anger and belligerence toward them. All hell had broken loose in my soul, and I was given over to the full extent of my anger and desire to punish and take revenge. What was going on? How could I possibly be so godly one moment and so devilish the next?

This may seem like a benign and slightly humorous report of something many of us experience quite often in difficult traffic situations. Perhaps you are not alarmed by my sin, but you should be. I have been a Christian for forty-six years, and I am still capable of shocking hatred and bitterness toward others, even toward the people I love most. My outward actions may be sanitized and under control most of the time, but my heart is full of riotous thoughts and feelings that reveal my deep capacity for selfishness, hatred, envy, pride, and every other sin imaginable.

I may read the Ten Commandments and feel smug and proud of my outward obedience, but when I contemplate Jesus' application of those commands in the Sermon on the Mount, I am undone. When Jesus shows me that sin is not just an outward phenomenon, but that true obedience must originate in the heart and flow outward, I realize that I am in big trouble. I cannot control my heart.

John Newton understood this dilemma. He wrote the following, not as a young and immature believer, but as a well-respected pastor and mature Christian: "This evil is present with me: my heart is like a highway, like a city without walls or gates. Nothing so false, so frivolous, so absurd, so impossible, so horrid, but it can obtain access, and that at any time, or in any place: neither the study, the pulpit, or even the Lord's Table, exempt me from their intrusion."[2]

Are you shocked by the alarming honesty of this man? What John Newton is saying is that he is capable of horrendously sinful thoughts, even while he is in the middle of his holiest activities, like writing sermons, preaching, and even serving the Lord's Supper. In fact, he highlights the contrast between his words, which he compares to the treble line in a piece of music, and his thoughts, which he likens to a jarring and discordant bass line. People who hear only the treble line may be impressed by his holiness, but the Lord hears the whole tune, in all its ugly confusion.

Sit with that shocking thought for a moment and consider its implications. Newton goes on to exclaim how astonishing it is that someone who knows as much of God's grace and mercy as he does should cherish and cling to the evils he finds himself attracted to. He should recoil from those temptations in the same way that he would if someone put a frog or a snake in his bed. And yet he found himself continuing to embrace them, which led naturally to Newton's conclusion: "Surely the person who finds himself capable of this, may, without the least affectation of humility (however good his outward conduct appears), describe himself as less than the least of all the saints, and the very chief of sinners."[3]

THE UNVICTORIOUS CHRISTIAN LIFE

This struggle may feel familiar to you as you wrestle with your own heart. If so, you are not alone. Newton suggests prayer and Bible reading as common examples for all of us.[4] We believe that the Bible is the Word of God and we admire the profound depth of the doctrines contained there, the grace of the precepts, and the richness of the promises and beauty it contains. With King David we might honestly say that it is sweeter than the honeycomb and far more desirable than silver and gold. At the same time, we often find our hearts and minds far more drawn to a good novel or magazine than we are to the Scriptures. The great privilege of reading the Bible frequently dwindles into a task that we are glad to be done with or overly pleased that we have accomplished!

Likewise, we think that prayer is a high and lofty privilege. It is an amazing honor and delight that the great Creator of the universe would stoop so low to lend a gracious and attentive ear to listen to the concerns and cares of his sinful and rebellious creatures. Yet though we love the idea of prayer and heartily recommend it to others, we ourselves spend very little time actually doing it. We will often forget God altogether throughout our day, only remembering that he is there when we find ourselves in extreme need. If we do manage to set aside time to pray, we are easily distracted at every moment, our minds drifting about and wandering to trivial things and endless lists of what we want God to do for us. At times our greatest joy in this discipline will be that of being able to check it off our list for the day and being able to say we have done it. Should God grant us the desire and ability to pray, we are likely to feel superior to those who confess a weakness in this area.

This same ongoing battle with sin is what the apostle Paul described in Romans 7, where he states that the things he wants to do, he can't do, and the things he doesn't want to do, he does (Rom. 7:19). His desires have been transformed so that he loves God's law and wants to obey it, but something else is at work in him that makes him feel as if he is a slave to sin (7:23). Paul concludes this passage with a cry of despair mingled with hope: "Wretched man that I am, who will deliver me from this body of death?" to which the answer is, "Thanks be to God through Christ Jesus our Lord!" (7:24–25). Paul is free to be alarmingly honest about his weakness because he is radically confident of the power and love of his Savior. The hope of heaven could never rest in him, even after many years as a Christian: it would have to come by the obedience of someone else on his behalf. As he faces up to the reality of his besetting sins, Paul does not conclude, "I'll just have to read my Bible more and try harder," even though as a Pharisee he had earlier exhibited far more willpower than any of us possess. Instead he casts himself on the mercy of God and looks to his rescuer to deliver him from his own sinful flesh—if not completely in this life, then surely in the life to come.

Many Christians think that believers should not struggle with ongoing sin in this way. They understand, correctly, that the Holy Spirit indwells all believers at the moment of their regeneration. Yet they do not have an accurate understanding of what the work of the Spirit looks and feels like in real life. They imagine him as some type of Holy Toolkit, implanted in their soul to be used appropriately for the purposes of sanctification. So you will hear people say things like, "You must allow the Spirit to work in you," as if there were an alternative. Others will say, "You must submit to the Spirit in order for him to bless and grow you," or "You must apply the Holy Spirit to your particular problem or struggle"—as if there were a switch in your heart you could turn on in order to activate or motivate him, and it is up to you to be willing and able to flip that switch more and more each day.

All of these sayings reflect the common view among many Christians that sanctification must be a cooperative effort between God and each believer. Even among those who believe that God does everything that is necessary for our salvation, many seem to think that he leaves our growth in sanctification to us. We will progress as far as we are willing to obey and initiate that growth, but we will remain immature if we are weak and disobedient or are unwilling to cooperate or work hard on our holiness.

What if the truth about us as believers is so much worse, yet so much more wonderful than you've imagined? What if God has left you in such a weak state here on earth that you couldn't even want to flip that Holy Spirit switch (if there were such a thing) without his help and enabling? What if he has done this very thing for our own good—and for his glory? What if the pathway to huge, overwhelming, and abundant joy in Christ does not take us around our sin, but takes us right through the middle of it?

This view, which is the view of sanctification that Newton held, is quite contrary to the "victorious Christian life" view that is taught in many churches today and portrays us as successful soldiers, conquering our sins and getting better and better with each passing day. Yet as we dive into Scripture, we will see that Newton's view of Christian weakness is utterly biblical and consistently taught throughout the Bible. Furthermore, it has historically been held by many great theologians and pastors in church history, and it flows through the Reformed confessions of faith and the writings of many godly Puritans.

Perhaps this truth does not inhabit the pulpits and self-help books of our day because it exalts the power and work of almighty God and deals a serious death blow to human spiritual pride. Nonetheless, it is truth that comforts weary and troubled believers who, like Newton, are able to admit that quite often they love their sin and really don't want to give it up. It also ushers believers into a life of joy and peace in this life that otherwise would be hardly imaginable. This joy and peace comes because it reminds us that God will have his way with us in spite of our weakness and the power of our ongoing sinful desires. Joy will never come by denying our deep sinfulness; rather, it must come by seeing how huge our sin really is and how completely it has been dealt with in Christ. Later in this book we will see why it is so important to understand our weakness and sin, how accepting our weakness can actually make us stronger, and what the connection is between weakness and joy.

For now, though, you need to know that your soul is still very sick, but you have a Great Physician who has promised to make you whole and is working in you every moment of every day. You are very weak, but you have a strong and perfect Champion who has won the battle against sin for you, and he now fights it with you. You are still prone to wander, but you have a Great Shepherd who always pursues you and brings you back, carrying you home in loving arms. You have a heavenly Father who would never let this sin and weakness remain in you if he did not plan to overrule it for your good and for his own glory. Praise God, you have the perfect High Priest advocating for you, praying for you, and holding on to you with a sure, steady, and loving hand.

GOD USES WHAT HE HATES TO ACCOMPLISH WHAT HE LOVES

Everybody knows that God hates sin.[5] In fact, it may be the only thing that some people know about God. The first chapter of Romans reminds us that God is angry at sin, and he has every right to be. He has given each human being irrefutable proof of his existence, his eternal power and divine nature, making it plainly visible to them in creation (Rom. 1:18–20). We have absolutely no excuse for our failure to fall on our knees before him every day in worship and adoration. However, not only do we fail to worship him as we should, we also actively suppress what we know to be true about God. This is no passive omission, but rather a determined and settled decision to exchange the truth of God for a lie and worship created things instead of the Creator (Rom. 1:25). It may not be a conscious and obvious decision to us each day, for by suppressing the truth we drive it underground into the recesses of our thinking, until our sin feels like no rebellion at all. But, rest assured, there is high treason involved. We are not sweet innocent infants throwing childish tantrums every now and then. We are beggars who have been given riches beyond imagination, who grasp those gifts greedily while refusing to thank or even acknowledge the Giver, instead shaking our fists in his face. In our addiction to sin, we resemble Satan far more than we display the image of God. Like him, we not only go astray ourselves but also tempt others to join us in our rebellion.[6]

Furthermore, we worship and idolize those good things that God gave to us as though they were gods, and we give our lives to them (Rom. 1:25). This is ugly, senseless, and destructive, and the Bible calls it sin. From the beginning of time our Creator has told us that he is the Maker of all things and that he alone has the right to determine right and wrong and to tell us how we should live in his world. Sin is therefore not just our wicked thoughts and actions that break God's laws; it is not just failing to meet up to God's expectations for us; it is a posture and a commitment to turn away from the living God to run after other things and bow in worship to them. God hates sin and told Adam that the consequences of sin would be death (Gen. 2:17).

Scripture uses vivid and terrifying language to describe God's hatred of sin and his holy and righteous determination to punish those who commit it. Old Testament episodes like the overthrow of Sodom and Gomorrah (Gen. 19) and the destruction of the Canaanite inhabitants of the Promised Land for their iniquity (see Gen. 15:16) serve as vivid reminders of God's power and willingness to judge evil. The Israelites themselves felt that same anger when they rebelled in the wilderness (Deut. 9:7–8), and their lengthy history of sins led to their exile from the land God had given them. According to Exodus 34:6–7, God's wrath is as much a part of his character as his grace and mercy are. Nor is this simply an Old Testament perspective; Jesus himself spoke of the wrath of God that remains on all those who do not believe in the Son (John 3:36). God hates sin, and nothing we say about the grace of God undermines or contradicts the truth of this fact.

GOD ALWAYS GETS HIS WAY

God is also completely sovereign over man's sin. From the first sin in the garden onward, Scripture shows us a Creator who hates sin but has never once been surprised or caught off guard by the wickedness of his creation. If God chose believers to belong to him in Christ before the creation of the world (Eph. 1:4), then long before Adam and Eve arrived on the scene the gospel had already been written. God is not up in heaven scrambling to patch up the naughty choices of the people he has made. God always gets his way, everywhere and in everything. Not one molecule in this universe operates outside of his will, not one cell divides without his permission, and no human thought startles him or escapes his notice or will. God made Adam morally perfect yet able to sin, and God permitted the intrusion of the serpent into the garden to tempt the first man and woman. Nothing in this story was out of God's control. He did not look down from heaven wringing his hands and wondering what choices Adam and Eve would make. God ordained the fall.

We also know, without a doubt, that God is not the author or inventor of evil. Everything that God created in the beginning was good (Gen. 1). God did not create sin, but God did ordain that sin would enter the world. Whatever a sovereign God allows, he has in fact ordained. This may be a troubling thought to some people, but there is no escaping this truth. If God can stop something from happening and he doesn't stop it, then he has ordained that it should happen.

We see this truth operating throughout Scripture. Notice, in the book of Job, who initiates the discussion that leads to Job's catastrophic losses (see Job 1). The scene is jarring: All of the angels are presenting themselves before the Lord. It looks like angel accountability and inspection time as they appear before the boss to answer to him. There is nothing surprising about that, until we read that Satan is among them! Wait a minute—what is he doing in heaven? What is he doing talking to God? The answer is that he too is one of the angels—a wicked, twisted, and evil one to be sure, but a created being who must also appear before the boss. The Lord asks him where he has come from, and he replies that he has been roaming through the earth, going back and forth in it. Then God drops the seemingly casual remark that gets the ball rolling, "Have you considered my servant Job, that there is none like him on the earth, a blameless and upright man, who fears God and turns away from evil" (Job 1:8). It appears that Satan hadn't particularly noticed Job before, but now that God mentions him, he is center stage and the action begins. With every twist and turn in the story, Satan must have God's permission to act (see 1:12; 2:6). At each point, God decides and decrees exactly how far Satan can go. God is not causing Job's suffering, but he is allowing it, ordaining it, and measuring it out in carefully prescribed doses according to his will.

We also see God's sovereignty over man's sin in the story of Joseph (Gen. 37–50). This tragic story captures our hearts with all of the profound suffering caused by the sinfulness in one family: an unwise father who openly favors one child over others, a prideful young man who enjoys the attention, jealous brothers carried away by their own evil desires. This story is ready for prime-time drama, complete with seductive temptress and jealous husband! There are also so many seemingly coincidental events that contribute to the way the story plays out: the random man in Shechem who just happens to know where Joseph's brothers have gone (Gen. 37:15–17) and the conveniently timed caravan going down to Egypt (37:25), amongst many others. For a long while these coincidences seem to be working against Joseph so that all hope seems lost, time and time again.

Yet at the remarkable end of the story, when Joseph does the unthinkable and forgives his brothers for their treachery, he makes a bold and audacious claim: "You meant evil against me, but God meant it for good" (Gen. 50:20). At each moment, wicked sinners were freely choosing to sin according to their own nature and desire, but God was sovereign over it all. He was sovereign over the thoughts that appeared and took a foothold in the brothers' minds, sovereign over young men abusing their brother, sovereign over the schedule of caravan drivers and the sexual desires of Potiphar's wife. In the process God allowed a great deal of sin to take place—sin which he hated but would overrule for good in the end. As Joni Erickson Tada says, "God has determined to steer what he hates to accomplish what he loves."[7] We will continue to see the truth of that statement unfolded throughout Scripture. God is completely sovereign over the sin of man and uses it to accomplish his perfect and holy will. What a mighty, surprising, and amazing God we serve!

Nowhere is this truth more powerfully and astonishingly displayed than at the cross, where the beloved and adored Son of God was tortured and killed. Do you think that God hated seeing Jesus mocked, beaten, and nailed brutally to a cross for crimes that he had never committed? I guarantee you that he hated it. How much self-control do you imagine it took for him to keep from intervening? How much grief do you think ripped his heart, and how much anger and rage must he have felt toward sinful men? Yet God did not break into history to end the insanity. Instead he ordained it and allowed the wicked ideas of sinful men to prosper and succeed. People had tried to arrest and hurt Jesus many times earlier but couldn't because his time had not yet come (e.g. John 10:31–39). Those were moments when God restrained human sin. He did not let those people sin as they desired. We aren't told exactly what happened or how Jesus escaped, but God intervened because it wasn't yet time for Jesus to suffer. But finally a day from hell dawned that would lead countless redeemed souls to a secure eternity in heaven. On this day, God stood back and did not restrain those who sought to crucify their Creator because, as Peter tells the Jews in Acts 2:23, "This man [Jesus] was handed over to you by God's set purpose and foreknowledge; and you, with the help of wicked men, put him to death by nailing him to a cross" (NIV). God ordained something unspeakable and horrible for himself and for his precious Son—the outworking of sinful purposes—because they both loved what it would accomplish.

GOD USES YOUR SIN TO ACCOMPLISH HIS WILL

The things we have discussed so far may be new to you, or doctrines that are old friends. Yet God's sovereignty over sin is not merely an interesting philosophical speculation to contemplate. We can see how God has acted in the great events of redemption to rescue his people both from and through the sinful acts of their enemies. Yet this is also a powerful doctrine for you today. Do you realize that just as surely as Satan needs God's permission to sin, so do you? God never tempts you to sin (James 1:13), but he is nonetheless in complete control of the sins that you do and don't commit, and he will just as surely use them to accomplish what he loves—your spiritual growth. Think back to the past week, or even the past few hours. Think specifically about the sins that you have committed and your reasons for doing so. You certainly made choices and followed your own sinful desires, yet at each point, God allowed you to sin.

One of the ways to see that is to think about some of the times in your life when you wanted to sin but God didn't let you. Perhaps you had sinful desires in your heart, but God restrained you by ensuring that you lacked the opportunity to sin in the way that you sought. Yet at other times, when God could so easily have prevented you from sinning through different circumstances, he allowed you to fall. God has been writing the story of your life and, on a grander scale, the history of his people by allowing and restraining sin. You are not a free agent, able to do whatever you want in the spiritual realm, any more than you are able to fly simply by wishing for some wings. You live under God's rule and nothing about you ever escapes his notice or evades his will. It is a transforming thought to look back on your life and realize that at each point where you sinned—and that would be many times each day—God allowed you to do so for his good purposes. He does not love your sin, tempt you to it, or cause it in any way, yet by permitting it, he ordains it for your good and his glory.[8]

Perhaps you are wondering how God can ever use our sin for his glory or our good. How can something so evil and hateful have a good outcome? We will discuss this more fully in the chapters ahead. For now, though, notice this. On the day that I met Edward in the grocery store and learned of his dental adventures, I experienced both the sublime joy of what God can do in my life and the ridiculous ugliness of what I am like apart from him. As I busily rushed through my day, thinking only of myself and what I wanted, God intervened. He invaded my mind with new truth from his Word and gave me ears to hear it. He then walked me into an experience of my fallen world and, quite contrary to my normal patterns of anger and selfishness, he gave me a moment of love for someone I would usually avoid and disdain. Then, so that I would not become proud and puffed up, God turned me back over to myself to discover, once again, what I am like apart from his rescuing grace. That minute of love for Edward was his gift to me and his work in me. In the very next minute, I received another gift from God: the clear and undeniable knowledge that unless he gives me fresh grace every minute of every day, sin is still what I do best.

How does that truth glorify God and benefit me? If I think I am cooperating with him in this joint pursuit of holiness, how can I not take some of the credit for my progress? Yet if I recognize that I am a saint one minute and a wretched sinner the next, I can see more clearly that all of my obedience comes from him and that without him I can quite literally do nothing. The Holy Spirit is not a switch you can turn on or off; he is not a tool you can choose to apply or ignore; he is not a copilot sitting beside you, ready to help if you really need him. He is the holy, powerful, active Spirit of the Living God, and he will always have his way with you. He is always at work in you, with or without your cooperation or permission, shaping you according to his will and his agenda. Sometimes he grants you fresh grace and power for obedience to show you what he can do in you, and sometimes he turns you over to yourself to discover how weak, helpless, and sinful you still are in yourself. Either way, he is always actively at work in you for God's glory and your own good, and that of his body, the church. Now if that isn't a fresh and glorious reason to fall down and worship him once again I don't know what is!

FOR FURTHER REFLECTION

1. When was the last time you behaved as a saint? What were you thinking and doing? When was the last time you behaved like a sinner? Describe this situation too. What made the difference?

2. Read Romans 7:14–25. Does Paul's struggle with remaining sin sound familiar to you? Do you feel unable to do the things you want and find yourself doing what you don't want to do? Describe how this works its way out in your life. Does Paul's honesty comfort or upset you? Why?

3. Read Psalm 139. Do you believe that God always gets his way in the universe? Does this thought comfort or unsettle you?

4. What has God been using to change you recently? In what ways has he used your own sin or that of others to teach you new things and help you grow?

5. When did God last stop you from committing a sin you wanted to commit? How did that make you feel?

6. In what unexpected and confusing ways is God getting his way in your life right now? What are you tempted to believe about God as a result?

7. Looking back over the course of your life, how has God used your sin and that of others to direct the path of your life? What about the lives of your friends and family members?

CHAPTER SEVEN

discovering your depravity

But that we are so totally depraved is a truth which no one ever truly learned by being only told it. —John Newton[1]

I could hardly believe the words which had just poured out of my mouth! If you had asked me one short hour beforehand if I was a racist, I would have been deeply offended. I was born in Jos, Nigeria, to missionary parents and had grown up in several different countries surrounded by people of all skin colors and nationalities. I knew I could justly be accused of all sorts of crimes, but racism simply wasn't one of them. However, as I marched down the charming, cobbled street in a dazed fury, I began to wonder.

At this particular point in our lives, my husband was planting a church in Oxford, England, and I was looking for a bed and breakfast where we could house a large team from one of our supporting churches in the US. I had visited several B&B's that day unsuccessfully and was feeling discouraged. If I couldn't find a place, we might have to host fifteen people ourselves! What a terrifying thought!

I knocked on a beautiful wooden door with stained glass in the middle and gazed hopefully at the well-kept garden and building. The door was opened by a woman wearing a sari and a veil and sporting a black dot in the middle of her forehead. She smiled politely and proceeded to give me a tour of her lovely facility. It was clean, well decorated, reasonably priced, and empty. As I looked at the bedrooms, I realized that if this lady would move one extra bed into a different bedroom, it would suit our needs perfectly. This seemed like a reasonable request to me, but the hostess protested. It couldn't possibly be done. I asked a few questions as to why it couldn't be done, but she was unyielding and adamant. I offered to help her move the bed, wondering if she was concerned about the mechanical difficulties. She shook her head no, and became slightly agitated. Now I was getting angry. I pointed out to her the obvious financial advantages of accommodating my request, since her establishment was completely empty and our business would bring her a great deal of income for two weeks in an off-season time.

Now she began to raise her voice at me and speak in a language I couldn't understand. I tried to calm her, but she had become irate and her fury poured out as she began to corral me toward the front door. This lady was kicking me out of her house! I couldn't believe it! My frustration bubbled into rage as she marshaled me past the threshold. Then it happened. In my outrage I looked her in the face and shouted at the top of my voice, "Oh, go home!" before I slammed the door in her face as hard as I could. That's how I discovered that I am a racist.

My anger turned to bitter shame and surprising hilarity as I headed home that day to begin my search again. I was living in this country for the purpose of helping to plant a church, but instead of being a beacon of God's love, I had gushed hatred and bitterness in the face of this lady. In a moment of extreme emotion and unguarded anger my heart had been revealed, and I rested all my rage on the color of her skin, the fashion of her clothes, and that dot in the middle of her forehead. Deep down in my heart, I had decided that this lady was stupid and unreasonable because she was a foreigner. I knew I couldn't excuse myself with platitudes like "Oh, I didn't really mean it." I meant every word of it. I knew that the words that escape our well-guarded lips in moments of weakness and stress demonstrate what we really think and who we really are. I was a bully—and a rude and arrogant one at that.

Laughter struck me when I realized that this lady had probably lived in the UK much longer than I had. She was likely a citizen of the UK, and yet I, an American on a visitor's visa, had shouted at her, "Go home!" Who did I think I was?

I am ashamed to admit that I never had the courage to go back and ask that lady's forgiveness. I wish I had. However, God did give me the grace to wrestle with my heart before him, to confess my disgusting sin and find forgiveness in my Savior who left his wonderful home and became an abused foreigner and alien upon this earth in order to rescue me from sin and give me an eternal home. How I came to thank him each time I would remember this embarrassing incident!

EXPERIENCE IS THE LORD'S SCHOOL

What was the Lord up to in all of this? Why did God ordain such a day for me? John Newton would not have been surprised by this event. He would have explained my outburst as another lesson in what he calls "the Lord's school of experience," in which we learn our lack of wisdom through making mistakes and our lack of strength by our slips and falls into sin. This is the way, he reminds us, that God weans us from our delusion that we have wisdom, power, and goodness in ourselves. This is how we learn the truth of Jesus' words, "Apart from me you can do nothing" (John 15:5).[2]

My loving heavenly Father wanted me to see in my own life the truth of the biblical statement that I am prone to exchange the truth of God for lies and to live in willful blindness to my own sin while I worship created things instead of the Creator (Rom. 1). My heart was lost in worship that day and I didn't know it. I worshiped the idol of comfort: I did not want to do all the hard work of housing this team. I worshiped the idol of money: I wanted the cheapest deal so that the budget would work. I worshiped the consumer values of my culture and sought to impose them on a person whom I perceived to be inferior and less intelligent. I worshiped power as I sought to bully her into doing what I wanted. Many idols had a firm grip on my heart at that moment, and I was clueless until those evil words gushed out of me. I don't know about you, but I am very resistant to seeing myself accurately until the Holy Spirit walks me through a day like this—until he makes the depths of my sin visible to me through my emotions, words, and actions.

IN THE WILDERNESS

Like the Israelites of the Old Testament, I am blind to the depravity of my own heart until God takes me into the desert. What an incredible experience it must have been to live through the exodus and see God's mighty power and love displayed on behalf of his people. Imagine the horrible pain and oppression of slavery and genocide that they endured at the hands of the Egyptians, and then the puzzling events surrounding all of the plagues. How the Israelites must have rejoiced to see their persecutors tormented by their powerful, avenging God! What a roller coaster of emotions must have accompanied those hurried preparations for the first Passover: joy at the thought of liberation, fear at the display of so much power and authority, hope for a better future, and terror at the thought of all that could go wrong.

Then there was that dark and fateful night when the firstborn sons of Egypt died, and the chosen people of God made their hasty and terrifying departure, only to be pursued by Pharaoh's powerful army. The drama reached its pinnacle when God told Moses to stretch out his rod, and an entire nation watched in joyful amazement and disbelief as God parted the sea and led them safely through the same waters that he then used to crush their enemies. Perhaps they now thought their difficulties were at an end and they had only to waltz into the Promised Land and live happily ever after! What could possibly stop them now? But they had a wilderness to get through—a physical wilderness of suffering and difficulty, and the greater wilderness of their own sinful hearts.

We marvel at the fact that just days after witnessing such great miracles, the Israelites were complaining about thirst and fearful that God had taken them into the wilderness to die. Just three months later they made themselves a Golden Calf at Mount Sinai and chose to worship it instead of the one true God who had delivered them so powerfully. In the wilderness the Israelites were confronted by their own weakness and sin in vibrant Technicolor.

When God led them into suffering and difficulty, they couldn't remember what he had already done for them so miraculously. Fear blinded them, leading them to forget God's goodness and accuse him of evil. In the wilderness their sinful, idolatrous hearts were exposed for them to see and for us to learn from. When Moses failed to come back down the mountain in a reasonable period of time, the Israelites trusted in their own wisdom and fashioned a god for themselves. They didn't understand that the same pillar of smoke and fire that led them to victory would often also lead them into trials and difficulties to show them what was in their hearts. They embraced the God of strength, liberation, and promise, but utterly rejected the God who would also walk them through the valley of death.

I, too, have a heart just like that. I love God dearly and worship him fervently when he walks me through pleasant pathways of peace and joy. But I turn on him swiftly and viciously when he contradicts my will and ordains dry, frightening, and uncomfortable pathways for me. If he never took me into the wilderness, I would never know what was truly in my heart. I would easily deceive myself into believing that I love him well and am eager to submit to his will.

A WILDERNESS OF PAIN

God brought this lesson powerfully home to me early one morning, in the restless hours just before dawn. I was in the shower, once again, at 3 a.m. This particular migraine had lasted for hours and showed no signs of abating. The hours of throwing up had exhausted me and prevented me from digesting any of the pain killers I had taken. In a desperate effort to escape the maddening, throbbing pain, I dragged myself into the shower to feel the water against my head. It did nothing to stop the headache, but it provided a few moments of distraction and relief. The problem was that every time I got out of the shower and back into bed, the pain returned. This was now my third trip to the shower, and I felt the tension in my head and body escalating as I realized the pain was worsening and the nausea returning. I was at the end of my rope, and as I got back into the shower all hell broke loose in my soul. A powerful anger against God welled up inside me and accusations poured out as the tears began to flow. "God, I have begged you time and time again to take these headaches, THIS headache away, and you will not. Why? What do I have to do? Why won't you listen and why don't you care?" The great theology I had learned over the years just fueled my contempt. I knew God had the power to do all of his holy will. He could easily stop all my headaches, and I was left to wrestle with the fact that he simply would not do it, no matter how much I pleaded, begged, or threatened.

Suddenly a thought entered my mind, and I know it wasn't from me. *If God does all things for his own glory and for the benefit of the elect, then somehow this headache must accomplish both of those goals. It has to glorify God and be good for me in some mysterious way.* One thought led to another as the Holy Spirit invaded my mind to rescue my soul: *If God loves me—and I know he does, for he has proved it at the cross—then it is love that compels him not to give me my way in this. Why would a loving heavenly Father plan this for me today?*

I knew these were not my thoughts, because they were foreign and uncharacteristic of me. My habitual pattern of response to headaches had been bitter complaint and accusation, but this was something else altogether: truth upon truth that would lead to a whole new way of thinking. I began to pray and confess my foul anger to God. This wilderness experience of ongoing pain had led me to stand before him and shake my fist in his face with infantile rage. Why would he ever tolerate such irreverent, prideful, and sinful behavior? I'd been doing this for years, and yet I lived! He hadn't destroyed me for my audacity or beaten me for my impudence. My eyes were suddenly opened to the piles of sin cascading out of my heart against God because he would not do my bidding or let me have my way, and I was undone. My thoughts changed from bitter accusation to wonder and worship as I marveled at God's incredible patience with me. God had never promised me a pain-free life, yet I had assumed he owed me that very thing and hated him when he would not accomplish my will or act as my errand boy.

I turned off the shower, and as the water ran swirling toward the drain, something enormous and dark began to drain out of my soul. God had used the wilderness of this migraine, and the many before it, to open my eyes to something I had been blind to for many years. My posture before God had been one of entitlement and laced with endless demands. This information was new to me, but it wasn't new to God. He had always seen my heart and known what was there, yet he had lovingly waited until this day to open my eyes and show me the depths of my sin.

Once again, I was not left simply feeling wretched and terrible. The enormity of my sin had to point to something wonderful about my Savior. Jesus hung on the cross for this specific burden of iniquity and loved me as he did so. He chose to suffer the literally breathtaking anger of his loving heavenly Father in my place so that I wouldn't have to die for my sin.

A picture formed in my mind as I imagined myself standing before the cross of my dying Savior and shaking my fist in his face because he would not take my headache away. The ludicrous implications of this image melted my heart with sweet repentance and profound gratitude. I realized that I was certainly capable of such a malicious, selfish, and immature act, yet nothing I could do would ever separate me from the love of Christ. Furthermore, Christ not only died my death, but lived perfectly for me, suffering through the illnesses and pain of a human, body-bound existence without grumbling against God, accusing him, or sinning in any way. Then he erased my record of resentment and anger and gave me his righteousness.

Jesus too once asked God for something and didn't get his way. In the garden of Gethsemane he asked God to take away the cup of suffering from him and let it pass him by, but God did not answer that prayer (Matt. 26:39). Jesus did not respond with bitter accusations and threats. Instead he prayed, "Not my will but yours be done," and rose to walk into a kind of pain I will never know and could never endure. Without anger and recrimination he chose to suffer great agony, so that my vicious anger toward God would not destroy me. And now his record was mine, even though I still struggled with sins like anger and bitterness. What an amazing love Christ showed me to suffer so willingly, and what incredible love the Father demonstrated in allowing him to do so in my place. What a joyful surprise to discover how he bears with me now, walking me through the deserts he has planned for me and patiently suffering the injustice of my sinful responses in order to show me my heart and teach me about his love.

WHAT I LEARNED

I wish I could tell you that the headaches ended that day. It would be even more wonderful if I could tell you that I was never angry with God again! However, neither of these things came to pass. Instead of my anger toward God completely disappearing, I began to see how much more anger there was within me than I saw that night. God is kind and merciful, and he does not show us the truth about ourselves all at once. Instead, he appoints seasons and moments when he opens our eyes bit by bit so that we can bear it. The wonderful thing about seeing the scale of my anger was that once I saw it, I could confess it and ask God for the gift of repentance. When we live in denial about sin and do not see ourselves accurately, we can't really grow. We are paralyzed until the Holy Spirit moves to give us sight and then grants repentance in his time.

One more surprising blessing arrived with the gift of this particular headache on this night. The headaches did not end that day, but they changed dramatically. Migraines plus powerful anger are much more severe and painful than migraines without anger! I discovered that my strong negative emotions fueled my beating heart and throbbing head, making them so much worse. As my heart attitude toward God and his will was transformed, the headaches themselves grew less severe and more bearable.

The Holy Spirit also began to show me many ways in which migraines were actually good for my soul. Migraines humbled me and reminded me that I am just flesh and blood. They showed me time and time again that God did not need my help to run the universe. He could do it quite well with me flat on my back in bed. On any given day, I would think that what I had to get done mattered most, yet God showed me otherwise. I thought to myself that God wants me to do this and this and this today—all good things, like serving my kids and working in ministry. Then I would discover that what God had actually decided was best for that day was for me to have a migraine.

I grew to remember more frequently that if a migraine was his good will for me, it was also his good will for my five children and my husband as well. Through my headaches, God was teaching my children to be more compassionate toward people who suffer, and he was training my husband to serve his family faithfully even when work was demanding and far more rewarding than wife and child care. My struggle even revealed the idolatries of others in our household, which called for their confession and repentance. In other words, my migraines weren't all about me! God used them to accomplish his good will in many lives and in various ways. This affliction never seemed like a good idea to me, but his perfect will had appointed otherwise. He gradually gave me more grace to submit to that will and believe that he is kinder and wiser than I could ever be. I began to learn and believe that this was his loving will for me, not his mean or vindictive will.

If decreasing the total number of sins that I committed were God's primary objective, he would have kept me out of the wilderness. However, he led me into the wilderness to reveal my sin to me because seeing my sin is good for me and brings him glory. It is good for us to see our sin, because when we do, our Savior becomes dearer to us. When we are standing tall and strong we do not tend to look at Christ—we don't need him. But when we fall flat on our faces, overcome with sin and weakness, there is nowhere else for us to look but to the One who has died our death and lived the life we should have lived. God loves broken and contrite hearts, and we don't acquire those by living the victorious Christian life.

It is precisely within the context of all of this weakness and sin that our God invites us to lean upon his mighty arm and promises to guide us with unsleeping eyes and a loving heart. He says to us, "Fear not, for I am with you; be not dismayed, for I am your God; I will strengthen you, I will help you, I will uphold you with my righteous right hand" (Isa. 41:10). However, that strengthening isn't always strength for obedience; sometimes it is the more remarkable power to survive our weakness and worship Christ more joyfully because of it. Our God goes before us, and at his powerful Word, crooked things become straight and light shines into darkness. In all of our failure and sin, God's promises to his children stand steady and true: he will be our sun, our shield, and our very great reward (Ps. 84:11).

FOR FURTHER REFLECTION

1. In what ways have you been surprised by your sin lately? What are you learning about your capacity to commit sins you never thought you could?

2. What is the biggest wilderness of your life right now? In what ways are you tempted to sin against God when he keeps you in that wilderness? What are you learning through the wilderness experiences of your life?

3. How would your life be different if you were always able to remember God's kindness and faithfulness to you in the past?

4. How do you tend to think about God and respond to him in good times and when he answers prayer? How do you respond to him when his answers are no and his will feels painful and unbearable? Why?

5. What sins do you commit over and over again? How do you feel about being a repeat offender? How is God bearing patiently with you in spite of your sin?

6. In what ways are you angry with God? How do you express your anger? Why are you angry?

7. Does your sin tend to lead you to despair or joyful worship? Why?

grace to fall

The most wise, righteous, and gracious God often leaves, for a season, his own children to various temptations and the corruptions of their own hearts. —The Westminster Confession of Faith, 5.5 (slightly updated by the author)

I sat in my counselor's living room wondering how on earth I had gotten to this place in my life. When I first began to meet with Margaret, we were living in Cambridge, England, and I had two huge problems that troubled me greatly. I was extremely overweight, and I was an angry woman.

My weight troubled me the most, perhaps because it embarrassed me the most. I had struggled with weight issues all my life, but now it was out of control and I was bordering on real obesity. I remember the day when I decided to give myself over to the worship of food. Long ago, I had honestly faced the fact that I was fat because I ate huge quantities of food every single day. I could fool other people by eating in secret, but I couldn't fool myself. I have had a thyroid deficiency for most of my life, but as a medical technologist I knew this wasn't the source of my problem. The medicine was working just fine, but my soul was sick. I prayed harder about my gluttony than about any other sin in my life. I was a faithful member of weight-watching groups,

Christian and secular, yet I ate and ate. I was out of control and very angry that God would not answer my desperate prayers and give me self-control.

One day as I walked through the cookie aisle of my local grocery store, there was great bitterness in my soul. I was angry because I was lonely and living in a foreign country. I was angry because my husband seemed so content in his PhD studies while I labored at home with small children in anonymity. I was even angry because I had to shop for groceries when I was tired and would rather be at home reading a good book and eating cookies. I was most angry that all I wanted to do was eat. It was there in the magnificent cookie aisle that a toxic rage broke out in my heart. I remember distinctly the moment when I said to God, "OK, if you won't help me to control myself and lose weight, I will eat myself to death." There was no better place to carry out that childish threat than this particular aisle. If you have never experienced the sheer diversity and creativity of British cookies, it may be difficult for you to imagine. There were so many delicious, crispy little treats that were easy to purchase and hide away for secret binging! I kept my word and followed through on that vicious threat, and within two short years I was clinically obese and more miserable than ever.

My anger also troubled me. It seemed so out of proportion with the narrative of my life and with God's incredible kindness and generosity toward me. I grew up in a wonderful, loving Christian home. I was cherished from my earliest days, disciplined firmly and without abuse, and taught the Word of God by parents who lived out its truth in front of me every day of their lives. I have never been physically, sexually, or emotionally abused, and yet I found myself to be deeply troubled. Many people I know would give everything to have grown up in the kind of wonderful family into which I was born. We were all sinners, but of the common or garden variety. There were no unusual skeletons in our closets, just the profound shaping influences of ordinary sin.

Furthermore, I was married to a man I deeply loved and highly respected. He was kind and caring, an excellent father to our little ones and a blooming theologian and preacher. I was living in one of the most beautiful places in the world, and by the time I met Margaret I had three charming, healthy, and adorable kids. All of my life dreams had already come true at the age of thirty-two, yet the anger simmered within me and erupted frighteningly from time to time. When that anger started to affect my two young sons, I was undone. I didn't know why I was behaving as I was. In my anger I would yank their little arms just a bit too hard or yell at them with viciousness far beyond what the moment called for. There were no bruises or fractures yet, but I was sure there would be if I didn't get help.

I sat in Margaret's home and poured out my heart to her. I went on for quite a while as she listened compassionately and jotted down some notes. As our first session ended, she looked calmly into my puffy, reddened eyes and gave me a peculiar kind of hope. She said, "Barbara, God is going to pour his grace into you. He will either give you grace to change and to grow in these two areas of great struggle with sin, or he will give you the grace to stay the same and survive your failure."

I was caught off guard by Margaret's confident statement. I didn't know there were options in the grace department, but if there were, I certainly knew which kind of grace I wanted. I had no interest whatsoever in staying the same and surviving my failure, whatever that meant. I was all about change, and I was pretty sure that's what God would want for me. After all, I had memorized a slew of verses about putting off and putting on, about obeying God's law and running the race with all my might. Didn't God want me to get better and better every day? Wasn't sanctification all about sinning less and less?

I didn't know my own heart very well back then, and I didn't know God's heart either. I had no idea that I could want to obey God for sinful reasons. All I knew was that my fat embarrassed me and revealed the chaos of my soul to everyone at a glance. I hated this sin because I couldn't hide it. It stared back at me every time I looked in the mirror. It followed me everywhere I went, encasing me in a coffin of suffocating flesh. I wanted to impress people with my intelligence and wit, my knowledge and wisdom, but my fat kept people from seeing me and led them to judge me as the failure I felt myself to be. I also knew that I didn't want to damage my boys. I loved them so dearly and feared that my sin would ruin them forever. I was absolutely sure that God wanted me to stop sinning, yet I felt completely helpless to fight these two powerful besetting sins.

COOPERATIVE SANCTIFICATION

Like me, many Christians grow up in the faith believing that Christ died to pay for their sins but that sanctification is in practice largely up to them. One pastor recently wrote on a website that sanctification is 100 percent God and 100 percent us, which is not only poor math but (more importantly) poor theology. In this view, since God is, of course, doing his 100 percent perfectly, the reason you are failing or succeeding must be entirely you. It is not surprising that Christians make this mistake. The essence of human fallenness is a determined autonomy from God, and it appears in our lives in the form of countless self-salvation strategies. Our natural mode of operation is law-driven, even after our conversion. We default to that strategy time and time again rather than fall on our faces before God and plead for his mercy and grace. At the same time we are often afraid that if we tell others that sanctification is entirely God's work, there will be no reason for them to try. Nor is this an entirely unfounded fear, because there have been plenty of people in the history of the church who have erred by teaching that human effort is irrelevant in sanctification, with devastating consequences.

Growing up, I held firmly to the "Holy Spirit Toolkit" notion. I believed that if I could find the right technique or work up enough willpower, I could use or apply him effectively to my worst sins. However, my escalating sense of shame and frustration over my weight and anger was the beginning of a new work in my life and a new understanding of God's will for me. I had thought God loved a victorious and triumphant heart, but I began to learn that God loves a humble and contrite heart (Ps. 51:17; Isa. 66:2) and has many surprising ways of forming these attributes within his children.

I have heard many Christians say that God would never command something of us that we cannot actually do, but I believe that they are seriously (though sincerely) wrong. After all, God calls all men and women to believe on the Lord Jesus Christ for their salvation, and none of us can actually do that unless he gives us the gift of faith we desperately need (Eph. 2:8–10). He commands that we should be perfect as he is perfect, and not one of us will achieve this until we reach heaven (Matt. 5:48). He commands husbands to love their wives as Christ loves the church, which is surely a goal that is far beyond anyone's reach (Eph. 5:25). He likewise commands wives to submit to their husbands as the church is supposed to submit to Christ (Eph. 5:22), yet there is no wife that can claim she has done this with anything approaching perfection. Therefore, to look at all the imperatives in Scripture to pursue sanctification as if this were something in our power to achieve is a deadly mistake. No wonder there are so many miserable Christians who are discouraged by their weakness and devastated by their ongoing sin.

If Christians believe that they can actually live up to God's standard and should be achieving that goal better and better each day, then one of two things will happen in the face of the stubborn reality of our hearts. Either we must rewrite God's standards downward into something more achievable—a set of external rules and regulations that are (at least in theory) within our power to achieve—or, if we retain the searching intensity of biblical truth, we assume that God is very disappointed in us. Oh, we may still appeal to the need for God's grace and power, but it is only an appeal to God's power to help you succeed in overcoming temptation, and never to the grace to find tremendous joy and delight in the Lord in spite of mountains of sin that don't respond to our greatest efforts. Many Christians have never heard of grace that is sufficient to survive brutal failure in our performance and nonetheless enables us to find deep joy and peace in the righteousness of Christ.

A DIFFERENT PERSPECTIVE

The apostle Paul, however, describes exactly this kind of grace and its place in a very different paradigm of the Christian life. In 2 Corinthians, Paul says,

> So to keep me from becoming conceited because of the surpassing greatness of the revelations, a thorn was given me in the flesh, a messenger of Satan to harass me, to keep me from becoming conceited. Three times I pleaded with the Lord about this, that it should leave me. But he said to me, "My grace is sufficient for you, for my power is made perfect in weakness." Therefore I will boast all the more gladly of my weaknesses, so that the power of Christ may rest upon me. (2 Cor. 12:7–9)

Paul had a problem and he wanted God to take it away. We don't know exactly what the problem was, but it was connected to his flesh—whether that means his sinful nature or merely his humanity or some combination of both. We also know that whatever it was, it came through Satan and it came from God.

Paul pleaded with God three times to take this thorn away, and three times God did not do as he asked. This reminds us of Jesus in the garden of Gethsemane. Three times he too pleaded that the cup of suffering might pass him by (Matt 26:39–44), and three times he received the answer that he didn't want to hear. It is notable that after three requests, both Jesus and Paul concluded that God had indeed answered them, and the answer was no. Instead of continuing to pray, fast, make promises, or commit to more discipline, each one quietly accepted God's answer. Jesus got up and walked into hours of torture and abandonment by God, knowing that God's strength would be made perfect in his weakness and death. He trusted that God would overrule the horrendous sins of many people and use his Son's death for his own glory, for his Son's glory, and for the good of all his people.

Likewise, Paul serenely concluded that God had a good purpose in refusing his request, which is that he would see clearly that "My grace is sufficient for you, for my power is made perfect in weakness" (2 Cor. 12:9). He understood that the story of his life was never meant to exalt and glorify him; it was meant to point to another. If God had answered all of Paul's prayers and made him strong and triumphant in every way, we would still be marveling at what a wonderful person Paul was. Instead, God left him weak and sinful. Instead of removing Paul's thorn, he said, "No, Paul, I like you better with it."[1] Now we can't sit around and admire Paul. He was a great apostle, but by his own declaration he was the chief of sinners (1 Tim. 1:15), and by his own description in Rom. 7 he struggled to obey God and sinned repeatedly. Instead we are left marveling at Jesus Christ, who delivered Paul from his body of death by dying in his place. Jesus is the one we're supposed to be smitten with, the one whose beauty takes our breath away.

The writings of John Newton present us with this Pauline paradigm for Christian growth through weakness, rooted practically and theologically in the vast doctrine of God's complete sovereignty. Of course, Newton is not the only person in the history of the church to have noticed this paradigm: it is the paradigm found in the great confessions and catechisms that flowed from the Reformation in the sixteenth and seventeenth centuries. Yet perhaps because of his own personal history of sin, Newton explains the paradigm more clearly than anyone I know.

As we mentioned in chapter three, Newton begins by observing that God could have saved us and made us instantly perfect, since all things are equally easy for God and he does all of his holy will.[2] Instead, he chose to save us and leave indwelling sin in our souls to wage war with our new desires. Why would a kind and loving God do such a thing? How does that work for his glory and for our good? If God were interested in simply decreasing the total number of sins committed in the universe, he would never have made such a decision. As much as he hates sin, there must be something else he values so highly that it is worth the cost of sin's destructiveness. Newton argues that this greater goal is the fashioning of humble and contrite hearts in God's chosen people as, through their ongoing weakness and sin, they come to trust in themselves less and less and to trust and delight in Christ more and more.[3]

LESSONS FROM A BARBIE® DOLL

Think with me for a moment about a Barbie® doll. She is beautiful and multitalented, perfect beyond possibility or reality. Her hair is shiny and blonde, her facial features chiseled to desirable proportions and her figure so attractive. She pursues exciting careers as an astronaut, veterinarian, and ballet dancer while finding time to go surfing on the weekends with Ken®. She is altogether gorgeous, but she has one fatal weakness: her deformed feet! She cannot stand up on her own, but must be held or propped up at all times. Her creators had an important reason for designing her this way—the necessity of her wearing ridiculously high heels at all times (there are no Barbie® slippers). Her makers formed her in a particular way with a particular weakness because of their own purposes for Barbie's® life.

Obviously God's relationship to his creation is not exactly like a designer and his dolls. Yet in a similar fashion, God chose to leave us significantly deformed and imperfect after our conversion because he values something more than our sinlessness. Spiritually we remain weak and helpless, just as unable to stand on our own as Barbie® herself. Though our feet may not be crippled and deformed, our souls are sinful and rebellious. We are new creation and old sinful flesh dwelling together—two natures competing for our affections and allegiance. To be sure, these two natures are not equal in their opposition. We are indwelt by the Spirit of the Living God, and God always gets his way. Our sinful hearts are no match whatsoever for his power and ability to work in us, with or without our permission.

We see this more clearly in matters of salvation. If the God of this universe chose you to worship him before the foundation of the world (Eph. 1:4), then you will not be able to resist his will. Those whom the Father has given to the Son are his sheep and no one can prevent them from coming to Christ, or subsequently snatch them out of his hand (John 10:27–29). God does this transforming work of salvation by making Christ so beautiful and irresistible to you that your greatest desire becomes worshiping him, and you may even believe it was your idea in the first place. There is no conflict between our wills and God's will in salvation because God sovereignly changes the wills of those whom he chooses to save so that we freely desire to come to him, something we would never have desired if left to ourselves.

POWERLESS TO STAND

It is exactly the same way with our sanctification. At the moment of your salvation, God began a new work in you that he has promised to complete, and over which he is sovereign every step of the way (Phil. 1:6). Jesus Christ doesn't start a new work in someone and leave it up to the individual believer to determine how it will go. He is ordaining and accomplishing all the details and means by which his will is carried out. The Holy Spirit is giving faith, grace, and spiritual gifts in the measure that he assigns them (Rom. 12:3–6), and producing fruit according to his will and timetable (Gal. 5:22–23). Your life is his story and not your own.

God has ordained that, like Barbie®, you cannot stand spiritually on your own. You will never discover the "secret" of standing or have a spiritual experience that makes you able to stand by yourself for long periods of time. When Jesus says, "Apart from me you can do nothing" (John 15:5), he means it quite literally. The powerful and loving Holy Spirit of God who lives in you decides at each moment whether you stand or fall. Unless the Holy Spirit enables you to stand, you will continue to do what you do best, even as a Christian—you will continue to sin. Sometimes the Holy Spirit holds you up and shows you what amazing and wonderful things he is able to do in you. At other times, without tempting you, he leaves you to yourself to fall into sin.

Many of our spiritual mothers and fathers understood this principle far better than we do. For example, the Westminster Confession of Faith describes this work in its discussion of God's providence.

> The most wise, righteous, and gracious God often leaves, for a season, his own children to various temptations, and the corruptions of their own hearts, to chastise them for former sins, or to reveal to them the hidden strength of corruption

and deceitfulness of their hearts, so that they may be humbled; and, to raise them to a more close and constant dependence for their support upon himself, and to make them more watchful against all future occasions of sin, and for various other just and holy ends. (WCF 5.5, slightly updated by author)

Notice the central point of this affirmation: your kind, loving, gracious, and compassionate heavenly Father *often*—not just occasionally—leaves his own children to many temptations for a season. The Holy Spirit who lives in you is certainly able to keep you from facing temptation. In fact, we are taught to ask for this very thing in the Lord's Prayer: "lead us not into temptation" (Matt. 6:13). Likewise, the Holy Spirit is also able to lead you into temptation and cause you to stand victoriously in it (Jude 24), as we shall see in the next chapter. Yet the Westminster Confession points out that in order to humble you and make you more conscious of your utter dependence on him, God often leaves you to temptation and does not intervene to rescue you. God lets go of you, and you do what is still natural to you as a depraved sinner—you fall flat on your face.

In all of this, God does not tempt you to sin, cause you to sin, or abandon you in any way. He doesn't have to. He simply does not intervene to hold you up. Like Barbie®, you cannot stand without his powerful help. Unless he actively gives you the will and desire to obey him and the power to follow through on that desire, you will surely fall. Since whatever God allows he has ordained, this is an aspect of his specific sovereignty over every minute of your life. God is in control of the thoughts that are allowed to fly through your mind. He is in control of which ones gain purchase in your soul and become tantalizing to you. Sometimes God intervenes with powerful truth and rescues you from yourself, like he did for me that day in the grocery store. Sometimes he withdraws his power from you—without leaving you alone for a minute—and allows you to be utterly yourself, as I was with the drivers who irritated me. We are completely responsible for our sin, but all of our obedience comes from him.

BIBLICAL EXAMPLES

If this perspective on our sanctification is accurate, then we would expect to find many examples of it in the biblical text. Sure enough, that is exactly what we see. For example, it was the Holy Spirit who led Jesus into the desert to be tempted by Satan (Matt. 4:1). God did not just ordain that his Son would face temptation and then step back to see what Satan would think up; instead, he actively walked him into it and oversaw all the circumstances surrounding that temptation. Unlike Adam and Eve, who sinned in a beautiful garden full of food and companionship, Jesus, the second Adam, would face temptation alone, hungry, exhausted, and in the middle of a barren desert. He had every human reason to be dazzled by the wealth, power, and glory offered to him, but he withstood that assault and remained perfectly obedient. God's sovereign will was that his Son would stand in the face of temptation, keeping the law in our place, so that outrageous lawbreakers like you and me would receive his spotless record of righteousness as though it were our own.

In other situations, God's sovereign will is for men to sin. For example, in Ezekiel 38, the Lord describes the onslaught of the final enemy, Gog and his allies, against his own restored people. The passage declares,

> Thus says the Lord GOD: On that day, thoughts will come into your mind, and you will devise an evil scheme and say, "I will go up against the land of unwalled villages. I will fall upon the quiet people who dwell securely, all of them dwelling without walls, and having no bars or gates," to seize spoil and carry off plunder. (Ezek. 38:10–12)

The Scripture calls Gog's plan "an evil scheme," yet this too is part of the Lord's sovereign plan for the world. All sin begins with a thought and Satan is certainly skilled at presenting tempting thoughts to us. He may use various aspects of the captivating world that surrounds us, and his suggestions find a ready home in our depraved and corrupted flesh. Yet this passage reminds us that whether the immediate source of our temptations is the world, the flesh, or the devil, the thoughts that successfully tempt us to sin are still nonetheless entirely under God's sovereign control. God's sovereignty over Gog's thoughts is matched by his sovereignty over the individual thoughts that you and I have every day that lead us into our own "evil schemes."

TEMPTED, TRIED, AND OFT-TIMES FAILING

We see this principle at work in the story of David and Bathsheba (2 Sam. 11–12). David's sin did not come out of nowhere. It began with him failing to pursue his duty to lead his people into battle. This was, after all, why Israel had asked for a king in the first place (1 Sam. 8:20). The narrator of the biblical story tells us that this incident took place "at the time when kings go out to battle," and on this occasion, David sent Joab in his place (2 Sam. 11:1). Likewise, why was David on the roof of his palace at the precise moment when Bathsheba happened to be bathing? God could so easily have intervened and orchestrated things so that David never faced this temptation. After all, it could have been raining, or God could have given him a bad cold!

Even after he saw her, God could have intervened to prevent this temptation from bearing its bitter fruit. When David had a chance to kill Saul in the cave, God gave David the strength to resist the temptation (1 Sam. 24:3–7). In the following chapter, when he was tempted to wreak vengeance on Nabal's entire household for their master's folly, God sent Abigail to prevent his sinning in this way (1 Sam. 25:26). David had been kept from

giving in to temptation many times in his life. Yet on this occasion, David was not rescued from himself. He saw something
beautiful and desired it. On that particular night these particular
sinful thoughts gained a firm foothold in his soul and became
strong desires. James tells us that "each person is tempted when
he is lured and enticed by his own desire. Then desire when it
has conceived gives birth to sin, and sin when it is fully grown
brings forth death" (James 1:14–15).

There was death in the air that night. Much evil came from
David's sin: a woman was taken, a husband was murdered, and
a helpless baby was left weak and dying. What good could possibly come of all this evil, treachery, and deceit at the hands of
one who had tasted so richly of the goodness of God? Psalm 51
gives us a clue. This psalm that David wrote out of his personal
experience of sin and failure gives all of us rich insight into how
God produces in us the broken and contrite heart that he so loves
(Ps. 51:17). Perhaps David could have written this psalm in the
abstract, but surely much of the psalm's power comes from its
roots in David's experience.

There was also eternal life gestating quietly on that night of
sin and death, for the Messiah, the Savior of the world, would
come from the union that began with this very tale. The mighty
Redeemer who would defeat sin and death forever would himself
be born from a line of wretched, adulterous, murdering sinners,
descended from David and Bathsheba themselves. God ordained
sin on this dark night, and he would use it for his glory and the
benefit of all his chosen people.

We see the same pattern at work in the New Testament. In
Luke 22, Jesus and the disciples retired to an upper room to celebrate the Passover meal. As they ate and drank together, Jesus
changed the script of the age-old ritual in order to speak of his
own imminent suffering as their Passover Lamb. Jesus offered
them the bread, saying, "This is my body, which is given for you.

Do this in remembrance of me." After they had eaten, he gave them the cup saying "This cup that is poured out for you is the new covenant in my blood" (Luke 22:19–20). The apostles' minds must have been reeling and their fear escalating as their hero persisted in speaking about his death and suffering. Then Jesus spoke of his betrayal, devastating them all with the news that the betrayer was one of them! In the midst of this dark and solemn narrative a fight broke out. The King of Glory had humbled himself to serve these men and would soon die for them, but all they could think about at this moment was who would be the greatest in this new kingdom Jesus kept talking about.

Then Jesus turned to Peter and told him, shockingly, that Satan had demanded to have him and to sift him like wheat (Luke 22:31).[4] Peter's response was to declare confidently his own ability to stand with Jesus, even if everyone else abandoned him (v. 33). Yet Jesus then told Peter that he would in fact deny him that very night (v. 34). Notice the same pattern that we have seen before. We see Satan appearing before God to make his audacious demands and, once again, God giving Satan a real but limited amount of power. In the case of Peter, Jesus said, "I have prayed for you that your faith may not fail. And when you have turned again, strengthen your brothers" (v. 32). What an astounding statement of God's sovereign purpose to bring good out of sin! Jesus knew that God would not rescue Peter from himself that night. Despite his most ardent protestation, Peter would fall flat on his face. The powerful, brave, and courageous disciple who would take up arms against the soldiers who came to arrest Jesus, slicing off a man's ear, would dissolve into a coward in front of a little servant girl and deny even knowing his dearest friend (see John 18:10–27).

Notice too that when Jesus prayed for Peter, he did not pray that he wouldn't sin. Instead Jesus prayed that after Peter had sinned, his faith would not fail him and that he would strengthen his brothers (Luke 22:32). It was certainly a terrible sin for Peter to lie and abandon the precious Lamb of God in his hour of greatest suffering, yet God would once again use something that he hated to accomplish something that he loved. God had big plans to use Peter in a dramatic way to build his church, but Peter wasn't yet ready. He was too proud, too rash, too sure of himself, and far too abrasive and arrogant to minister gently and lovingly to weak and sinful sheep. He thought he was better than the rest of the disciples, declaring, "Lord, even if everyone else leaves you, I will never leave you!" (see Matt. 26:33). Peter needed to know his own sinfulness and need before he could care for God's flock with gentleness and humility.

Through that sin, God was up to something big in Peter's life. Peter needed to know the outrageous depths of the forgiveness that he himself needed and would receive in Christ so that he could then extend the same compassion and forgiveness to others. God certainly could have strengthened Peter to obey in that moment, but had he done so, the larger lesson would have been lost.

The same holds true for you and me. Does the story of my grocery shopping experience, along with the stories of King David and the apostle Peter, map onto the narrative of your life? Do you find yourself at times full of wonderful thoughts about God and able to do wonderful things for him, only to see yourself a short while later full of angry, bitter, and evil thoughts and sinning again? I find that this happens to me frequently on Sunday mornings, which ought to be the holiest times of my week! I begin Sunday mornings in a distracted and resentful state, rushing around to help with setup in our church and balancing sound for the music team. I don't really want to do these things, but I am called to serve and help in this way for now, so I set about these tasks most often with a grumbling heart. As the service begins, my cold, stony heart is often warmed and softened as I am called to worship and confess my sin before God and am assured of his pardon and love. Tears of joy and gratitude are frequent visitors—always against my will—and my soul is refreshed, strengthened, and empowered as we end with the Lord's Supper, rejoicing and celebrating the astounding love of our wonderful Savior!

Yet I often can't even seem to make it out of the gymnasium where our service is held before my heart plunges and I find my soul flaring. The minute my eyes are taken off Christ and placed back on myself, I am prone to struggle with all kinds of sin. I struggle to love people who complain about the service or have high expectations of me as a pastor's wife. I have difficulty forgiving people who don't keep their word and those who make commitments and abandon them easily. Since the gym is always chock full of people, it is usually full of such sinners, of whom I am quite sure that I am the chief. It comforts my soul, however, to know that in my weakness and sin I am not some kind of grisly aberration—I am not a spiritual monster. In the sovereign will of God, the Christian life is supposed to be this way. God is capable, when he pleases and for his own purposes, of giving me the grace to stand and resist temptation. But often he chooses instead, for his own good purposes, to show me grace through my falls, humbling me and teaching me my desperate need of him.

FOR FURTHER REFLECTION

1. In what areas of your life has God given you grace to change and overcome sin? In what areas of your life have you been left unchanged? How has he shown his grace to you when you don't overcome sin?

2. Do you believe it is up to you to cooperate with God in your sanctification in order to grow? Why do you believe this? Why are there times you won't cooperate with God?

3. In what ways have you tried to get the Holy Spirit to do what you want him to do, hoping that he will help you change?

4. Do you have any "thorns in the flesh" like Paul did? How do they make you feel? How many times have you prayed that God would take these thorns away? Why do you keep praying? What specific things has God been doing in you in the areas where his answer is still no?

5. In what ways has God caused you to stand lately and made you victorious over sins that ordinarily trip you up? What sins are you tempted to commit when God causes you to stand? Why?

6. In what ways has God turned you over to yourself and let you fall?

7. What sins are you tempted toward when God lets you fall again and again? Why?

8. Describe a time in your life when God changed your heart and mind and made you willing to do something you previously did not want to do. What does that teach you about God?

standing in Christ alone

*Though we can fall of ourselves, we cannot rise
without his help.* —John Newton[1]

think most Christians rightly believe that all our strength to
live the Christian life must come from Christ. However, we
may mean different things when we say that. Some people
believe that the Holy Spirit who indwells us at the time of salvation also constantly enables us to be obedient. In other words,
the grace received at conversion includes an abiding power to
choose to obey God whenever we are willing to do so. Therefore,
the willingness and strength to stand in obedience come from
our own diligence and hard work as we walk through life.

John Newton had a different view of Christian obedience—
one which places all the blame for sin on the sinner, but gives all
the credit for obedience to God alone. Newton connected this
with the idea of boasting and rightly concluded that if there
was to be absolutely no human boasting before God for good
works, then sanctification would have to be all of grace and 100
percent up to God.[2] Far from laying the blame on God for our
sin, however, Newton viewed the abiding presence of our fallen
sinful nature and the constant activity of Satan as explanation
enough for our indwelling and continuous sin.[3] He also reasoned

that, if this is true, only God can get the credit when his Spirit moves with a fresh act of grace to engage believers' will so that they want to obey, and then provides the actual strength to follow through in obedience.

In this, John Newton is echoing the insight of the historic Reformed confessions of faith. For example, the Westminster Confession says,

> Their ability to do good works is not at all of themselves, but wholly from the Spirit of Christ. And that they must be enabled thereunto, beside the graces they have already received, there is required an actual influence of the same Holy Spirit, to work in them to will and to do, of his good pleasure: yet are they not hereupon to grow negligent, as if they were not bound to perform any duty unless upon a special motion of the Spirit; but they ought to be diligent in stirring up the grace of God that is in them. (WCF 16.3)

Likewise, the Belgic Confession declares,

> So then, we do good works, but not for merit—for what would we merit? Rather, we are indebted to God for the good works we do, and not he to us, since it is he who "works in us both to will and do according to his good pleasure" (Phil. 2:13)—thus keeping in mind what is written: "When you have done all that is commanded you, then you shall say, 'We are unworthy servants; we have done what it was our duty to do.'" (Luke 17:10).[4]

Like Newton, the framers of these Reformed confessions believed that each specific act of obedience requires an actual influence of the Holy Spirit upon our hearts. The grace that we received at the moment of our salvation is not some sort of global enabling power that we must discover how to tap into and activate in order to grow and be blessed. On the contrary, it is the presence of the personal and powerful Spirit of the Living God who presides over our souls and decides at each and every moment whether he will give the grace to make us want to obey and whether he will also give the further grace for us to succeed in obedience.

This kind of specific and microscopic care for us as individuals should not surprise us. When Jesus spoke of the hairs of our heads being numbered, he was pointing to a kind of watchful love that is so comprehensive that a single hair cannot fall from our scalps without his permission (Matt. 10:30). How then could we ever imagine that God would leave the great and mighty business of our spiritual growth up to weak and sinful people like us? Surely the matter of which sins we will and won't commit is far more important to God than the number of hairs that we can call our own on any given day.

Likewise the tiny and fragile sparrow, whose demise at the paw of a neighborhood cat scarcely causes us a second thought, is the object of God's sovereign will (Matt. 10:29). How much more, then, will God exercise his sovereign and loving care over the sanctification of his children? Those whom God has made in his own image and redeemed with the blood of his only precious Son are far more valuable to him than little birds (Matt. 10:31)!

Other Scriptures also speak of God's personal attention being lavished on each of us throughout every moment of our days. He knows the words that are on our tongues before we speak them (Ps. 139:4), and he decides whether or not he will let them fly out of our mouths. He knows our thoughts (Ps. 139:2), and he knows the intricate characteristics of our sinful flesh. He is writing the history of the redemption of his people by restraining them from the sins that he will not allow and turning them over to the sins that he has planned to overrule for his glory and our good. What we plan for evil, he uses for good in spite of our worst intentions.

IS THERE NOTHING WE CAN DO?

Yet even though obedience requires a fresh act of the Holy Spirit each and every time, the Westminster Confession reminds us that we are not to use that as an excuse for giving up the struggle! This is a wise and necessary reminder. It is perhaps inevitable that when fallen human beings are faced with the discouraging news that they can't "just do it," some will conclude that their sin is therefore God's fault and they no longer need to try to live obedient lives. It seems that the apostle Paul was used to being asked this same question—"Are we to continue in sin that grace may abound?" (Rom. 6:1)—to which Paul's answer is "NO!" It may make sense to human wisdom that if sin somehow opens up the floodgates of God's mercy and unleashes fountains of grace, then we should sin more in order to get more grace. God's Word, however, says, "Absolutely not!" One of the saddest mistakes we can witness is when believers use God's patience, kindness, mercy, and grace as an excuse to sin rampantly and flagrantly. Even then, however, we don't need to panic or despair. Since the Holy Spirit completely governs which sins will and won't be committed, even the sins of his immature and misguided children will be used for his glory and their good.

Only God knows why he tolerates such "abominable frol-ics" (as Newton called them) from those he has rescued, but it is clear from Scripture that the beauty of the gospel is designed to make us want to obey Jesus more and more, rather than less and less. The radical forgiveness that we have in Christ allows us to live our lives with confidence and boldness even though we still sin a great deal every day. However, God's forgiveness is not meant to serve as a rubric for giving up and giving in to licentiousness, foul language, drunkenness, and sexual sin. When Martin Luther told Philipp Melanchthon to "sin boldly," he had in mind Philipp's recognizing the reality of his indwelling sin so that he would pray equally boldly for God's grace, not actively pursuing his sinful desires.[5] It saddens me greatly when I hear Christians broadcasting their bold sin in the name of grace and Martin Luther. The gospel leads us to deep grief over our sin combined with great joy in our Savior, but never to bold and rampant enjoyment of sin.

John Newton had no problem whatsoever in examining and proclaiming the complete inability of the believer to obey, and at the same time calling each one to work hard toward sanctification. For example, he says,

> It is, however, his command and therefore their duty; yea, further, from the new nature he has given them, it is their desire to watch and strive against sin; and to propose the mortification of the whole body of sin, and the advancement of sanctification in their hearts, as their great and constant aim, to which they are to have an habitual persevering regard.[6]

In another place he writes,

> It is a believer's privilege to walk with God in the exercise of faith, and, by the power of his Spirit, to mortify the whole body of sin, to gain a growing victory over the world and self, and to make daily advances in conformity to the mind of Christ. And nothing that we profess to know, believe, or hope for, deserves the name of a privilege, farther than we are influenced by it to die unto sin and to live unto righteousness. Whoever is possessed of true faith, will not confine his inquiries to the single point of his acceptance with God, or be satisfied with the distant hope of heaven hereafter. He will be likewise solicitous how he may glorify God in the world, and enjoy such foretastes of heaven as are attainable while he is yet upon earth.[7]

Though we remain in this life knitted to sinful flesh, full of weakness and utterly dependent upon God, and though we only make "small beginnings in obedience" (as Heidelberg Catechism Q. 114 puts it), we are also a new creation (2 Cor. 5:17)! The Spirit of God creates new desires in our hearts, and as he gradually reveals to us the breathtaking beauty of our Savior, he grants us a growing longing to be like him. Newton therefore calls us to work hard toward our growth while at the same time keeping in mind that without Christ we can do nothing. What might humanly seem contradictory fits together beautifully in the divine plan of redemption and sanctification.

In this, Newton was content to echo the notes sounded by the Bible. The Scriptures call us to run the race with all our might (1 Cor. 9:24) and fight the fight with all our strength (1 Cor. 6:12). We don't have to understand all the reasons God calls us to try so hard and yet allows us to fail so often, but we do need to submit ourselves to his wisdom and, out of love and gratitude to him, seek to obey his commands. Jesus said, "If you love me, you will keep my commandments" (John 14:15). Indeed, the more we see of the gospel, the more we grow in love and gratitude to Christ and the more steadily this desire should grip and motivate us.

THE BEAUTY OF TRYING WITH ALL YOUR MIGHT

I certainly don't know all the reasons God has ordained that we try hard and fail instead of doing nothing at all. Newton argued that God views even the weakest attempt that the Christian makes as glorious.[8] God loves to admire his work in us, and he loves to see his Son in us. If we don't try hard and still fail, we might delude ourselves into thinking that we could obey God if we chose to make the effort. Yet when we try hard and fail, and try hard and fail again, we truly learn to ascribe our entire salvation to the work of Christ alone.

I know a few things about trying hard. When it comes to fighting sin, I can deceive myself quite easily. There are some sins that, by God's kindness and grace, I don't find very tempting . . . at least not at present. It feels to me that I can beat those sins when I try. One example from my life comes in the realm of fantasy. As a younger woman, I frequently struggled with sexual fantasy and lust. This troubled me, of course, as it should. I heard a sermon once about putting on and putting off, whereby I was encouraged to put off the sin by putting on some sort of obedience. I noticed that I had in my Christian arsenal one powerful antidote to sexual fantasy—the memory of the days when I gave birth to each of my kids. That may sound humorous to you—what better way to avoid sinful thoughts of sex than by recalling the excruciating pain of childbirth! However, that's not exactly how this deal worked. The birthdays of my children are the happiest memories I have. They fill me with incredible joy, gratitude, and sheer delight. It is that joy and pleasure that are strong medicine against sin.

My youngest daughter, Rosie, almost died the day she was born. She suffered oxygen deprivation and entered the world with a purple hue to her skin. Once the doctors got her breathing they discovered she had suffered damage during the delivery and was paralyzed on the right side of her body. We were warned that this little one might not be healthy. It was likely that the paralysis would remain and possible that she would be brain damaged. Only hours before, a baby had died in the room next to mine. She had been stillborn, her heart rate suddenly disappearing without explanation. Why did my baby live while that child died? Not only did my child live, she went on to thrive— two weeks later the paralysis had disappeared and she was an energetic and sparkling little newborn. Today she is a bright and beautiful young woman, and I am often undone by the memory of what could have been. I didn't deserve to have my baby live and recover, and yet God was incredibly merciful to me. In that powerful memory of the joy of my babies, and especially Rosie, God gave me strong help against one type of sin.

Of course, I didn't realize that this mechanism was a gift. It seemed that all I had to do was flip a switch, play a tape in my brain, and the sexual thoughts would give way to better ones. It felt like I didn't have to try very hard. However, in his kindness, God gave me other battlefields where there would be no such illusion. He is a loving Father who knows that we are weak, that we are dust, and he is gentle with us. If every area of life were a battlefield, we would die of discouragement. Yet in his love God makes sure that all of us have one or two battlefields, at least, where no matter how hard we try to obey, we simply cannot succeed.

As I mentioned, my weight has been one of the most difficult and painful struggles of my life. For fifteen years, I was clinically obese. I tried everything I could to be obedient and faithful, and at times I seemed to stand in victory for a while. On four different occasions I lost 80 pounds or more on some diet plan, but each time I gained back more than I had lost until I was shredded with discouragement and shame. Grace to stand can come in many surprising ways. For many years I was determined to win this battle, while I imagined how people would admire me for my achievement and how I could then go on to teach others to do the same.

As it turned out, this was not exactly God's plan. Instead, God spent fifteen years proving to me that I couldn't do it, before he did it for me. Pride had driven me to try to do this on my own, but constant failure opened my heart and mind to avenues of help that had previously seemed too embarrassing. Finally, in 2002, in the face of high blood pressure and diabetes, shame and pride just didn't matter anymore, and I began to research the possibility of bariatric surgery. I was an unhealthy person and a spectator in the lives of my kids, so when my insurance agreed to pay for the surgery, I signed up. In this particular surgery, the stomach is stapled off until all that remains is a small pouch. The intestines are also shortened to reduce the calorie absorption capacity of the GI tract as food passes through, and dramatic weight loss follows. I guess you could say that my stomach offended me, so I had it cut out! Since then, I have had many, many reasons to thank God that my present size has almost nothing to do with me! It is a rich and undeserved blessing for which I thank God every day. I sometimes chuckle to think how my heavenly Father has made it impossible for me to boast about losing 140 pounds! I can't give advice to anyone else; I can only give thanks to God for his kindness.

One of the biggest problems I encounter in the counseling room is the normal human pride that keeps people from seeking and accepting help. Sometimes this comes from the misguided notion that God expects us to get our act together and obey on our own. It is so hard to understand that God loves humble and contrite hearts that have nothing to boast about other than the love of Jesus Christ. Pride keeps us isolated from others and often leads us to turn away from avenues of help that might be available, whether medical or community-driven. However, a long struggle with sin usually brings us to the end of ourselves, and only then are we ready to cry out to God for deliverance and look for help. God will quite often crush us with our weakness before he gives us the grace to stand strong—and he shows love to crush us. When our struggles with sin are brief and light, we may be grateful when they end, but only in proportion to the length of time of our pain and to the effort we have expended. Then, when we stand, we seek to take the credit for it ourselves. After all, it feels as if we did it ourselves. We don't spend much time thinking about Jesus in such cases because we didn't really need him much. Our eyes remain primarily on ourselves, and we eagerly tell others how we were able to overcome this sin.

But when we have wrestled with a besetting sin for many, many years and we still fail, things become much clearer. Then, when grace is given for obedience, there is much less confusion about who has done what. If I have tried with all my strength and failed, I finally become convinced that without Christ, there simply is no hope of victory. If victory comes at that point, I am more likely to understand, deep down in my soul, that Christ has made all the difference and delivered me in spite of myself.

John Newton observed that God seldom frees us from besetting sin before showing us how deeply inability is rooted in our souls. If this work were cooperative, with me and Jesus working together, then at the end of the performance there would be two people on stage taking the bow. However, understanding my inability leads me to a far different posture. I am not on stage next to Jesus, taking a bow. Instead, I am flat on my face in the dust, with my hand on my foolish mouth, worshiping at the feet of my beautiful Savior whose power and grace has rescued me.

Newton compares the struggle with besetting sin to a ship lost at sea in a storm. If the storm lasts for several hours or days, the sailors may be terrified and give themselves up for lost; their relief will be great when it ends and they sail safely into the harbor. When, however, a sailor has been lost at sea for a month and has counted himself lost for days upon end, how great will his relief be when he sails into harbor? How will his joy be different in magnitude and strength than if he had spent only a day or two in danger?[9] So it is with our struggles against sin. Some will be brief, and God will grant relief swiftly. Some will last for years and years, and we will learn that it is hard to need so much forgiveness over and over again. Most will remain in some form until we see him face to face, and then we will simply marvel that we can stand at all before this Holy God and his captivating Son. Yet, as we continue to sin much in this earthly life, we will know that we have been forgiven much, and our love and appreciation for the longsuffering nature of our God will become clearer. Newton declares that there is no other way to get a broken and contrite heart over our sin, or a compassionate and loving heart toward others, than to struggle a great deal with sin.

Thus it brings God glory and is good for us when we try hard to obey. The results of our efforts are in God's hands. Sometimes we will try hard and succeed, but quite often we will try hard and fail. The fact that the end result is up to God in no way diminishes the fact that we are called to work hard and run fast. Indeed, sometimes we won't even have the strength or desire to try at all. Then God's glory will be revealed in the fact that he holds onto us regardless and continues his work in us, enabling us, if not to leap and bound in the right direction, at least to crawl, or sometimes simply to face in the right direction.[10] Even then, his grace is still sufficient for our weakness.

GOD'S SOVEREIGN GIFT OF FAITH

We don't get to choose how strong our faith is or how far we will progress in sanctification before we stand before him face to face. In Romans 12, Paul ties together striving for growth and obedience with God's sovereignty in a remarkable way.

> I appeal to you therefore, brothers, by the mercies of God, to present your bodies as a living sacrifice, holy and acceptable to God, which is your spiritual worship. Do not be conformed to this world, but be transformed by the renewal of your mind, that by testing you may discern what is the will of God, what is good and acceptable and perfect. For by the grace given to me I say to everyone among you not to think of himself more highly than he ought to think, but to think with sober judgment, each according to the measure of faith that God has assigned. For as in one body we have many members, and the members do not all have the same function, so we, though many, are one body in Christ, and individually members one of another. Having gifts that differ according to the grace given to us, let us use them.

First, notice how Paul gives a strong call to obedience as he urges believers to offer their bodies as living sacrifices, holy and acceptable to God (v. 1). The imperatives are powerful and potentially crushing here. We are to be transformed, discerning and passionate in our pursuit of a holy life, putting our own desires to death in the process. Yet, at the same time, Paul reminds us of two things. As we strive hard, we will need to have our minds renewed, a process in which we are passive and God is active. Further, there is a strong call to humility and a reminder not to think of ourselves too highly, but to evaluate ourselves with sober judgment (v. 3). We are to think carefully about the fact that it is God who assigns what kind of faith we will have. We don't get to make that decision! God gives strong faith to some and weak faith to others according to his wisdom and plan, and we are to consider our own faith and that of others as we live together in one body. God has assigned varying amounts of giftedness and grace according to his will, not according to what we wish he would do. This is so contrary to the Disney delusion! We can't just try harder and be stronger; we can't even "just believe"! Rather, we must submit to God's will and work with the faith and gifts that he has ordained for us.

It is a devastatingly painful thing to be a weak Christian in the American evangelical church today. So much emphasis is put on reading, praying, growing, and victory that there isn't much room left for those God is holding on to with a strong arm, but who may know little of the joy of full assurance of faith and the satisfaction of growth in grace and obedience—at least in this life. What are we to do with those who have just enough faith to be counted as belonging to Christ, but who through the severity of life circumstances that God has assigned to them and the devastating effect of shaping influences, can hardly remember the gospel from day to day?

I am convinced that these believers—whom some may refer to as "the least of these"—may in fact be among the real champions of our faith. They limp through life barely able to remember the truth or connect the mighty doctrines of the faith to their struggles in a way that would calm their fears and quiet their hearts. They are told they must run toward God with all of their strength, yet often find themselves barely able to lie on the ground facing the right direction. They cling to God desperately, but without ever feeling an assurance of his presence or an ability to rest in the love that surrounds them. Shall we plan more Bible studies for them? Shall we discipline them when they repent time and time again but can't quite seem to break free from deeply ingrained patterns of sin?

I am convinced that these precious saints are among those Christ died for and are in their own way heroes of the faith, clinging to God in spite of the weakness of their faltering faith. They are the bruised reeds that we must not break and the smoldering wicks that our triumphalism would so easily extinguish (Matt. 12:20). They are the ones who believe in the face of their own struggles with unbelief (Mark 9:24). We must love them, bear their burdens gently, and help them to carry their loads, because they belong to us (Gal. 6:2). They are our family in the Lord.

I counsel many people who struggle with assurance and suffer with a faith that is weak. I just can't wait to see the joy in their faces when they finally get to heaven! Those who are blessed with strong faith in this lifetime will wake up to find themselves in glory just as they expected. They knew that it was all true, they trusted in God, and perhaps they rarely experienced a moment's doubt. For others, however, that moment of their awaking will be worth a fortune to watch. Can you imagine the surprise and delight on their faces to find themselves in heaven after all? On earth they could barely hope that the promises of eternal life were true and that God had actually saved them, and they never felt the joy of it during their lifetime. But once they get to heaven it will all change, and I imagine that they will perhaps spend the first millennium or two in heaven surprised and delighted simply to be there. I can only imagine their joy when they hear the words. "Well done, good and faithful servant. . . . Enter into the joy of your master" (Matt. 25:21). Their joy in heaven will be matched only by the Father's joy in proving once again that the gospel of his Son really is enough to save the weakest and most broken of people. The angels are already dancing and the band is playing for them; they just don't know it yet (Luke 15:7, 9, 22–24). God's grace really is sufficient for the least of these.

A WORD TO THE WEAK

If you are reading this and you feel weak, please be encouraged. I am speaking here to people who struggle desperately with fear, anxiety, depression, and doubt, and people who struggle repeatedly with sins that they think are beyond God's reach. Sexual sinners often feel this way, particularly Christians who battle feelings of same-sex attraction and the temptation to engage in homosexual sin. Although God did not create your struggle or tempt you to it, he has called you to walk with it. He has assigned it to you, and he loves you as he calls you to walk through it. He is not disgusted by you. There is no sin under the face of the sun that can surprise him or repel him from you. You are not the worst of the worst or more depraved than those who struggle with more socially acceptable sins such as gluttony, pride, or overachievement. Sin is sin, and we are all in the same mess regardless of the focus of our sinful desires. The roots of sin in the heart are all the same, even if the outward workings of those sins vary immensely. God often does his most breathtaking work in the context of struggles with what we consider the most shameful sins. Many of the godliest men I know are Christian men who struggle with same-sex attraction and strive to live in obedience to God.

If you are in Christ you are cherished, you are washed, you are clean, and you are wrapped up tightly in the perfect robes of his goodness. Wherever you have sinned and continue to sin, he has obeyed in your place. That means that you are free to struggle and fail; you are free to grow slowly; you are free at times not to grow at all; you are free to cast yourself on the mercy of God for a lifetime. Repeated failure does not mean that you are unsaved or that God is tired of you and disappointed. It does mean that he has called you to a difficult struggle and that he will hold on to you in all of your standing and falling and bring you safely home.

You have great reason to hope. God is faithfully at work in you and he does change his people. He may change your desires and relieve your battle, or he may give you peace and joy in the midst of thoughts and desires that don't change. Either way, he loves you the same way that he loves Jesus, and he is always for you and never against you. You too are a trophy of grace and will shine for all eternity in his heavenly showroom. You are one of the ornaments that will decorate the halls of heaven and bring glory to God forever. As Tullian Tchividjian put it:

> Because Jesus was strong for me,
>   I am free to be weak.
> Because Jesus won for me,
>   I am free to lose.
> Because Jesus was Someone,
>   I am free to be no one.
> Because Jesus was extraordinary,
>   I am free to be ordinary.
> Because Jesus succeeded for me,
>   I am free to fail.[11]

A WORD TO THE STRONG

Has God blessed you richly with gifts like emotional stability and mental health? If so, you may not often experience feelings of anxiety, depression, or shame, and you may be skilled at moving through life with purpose and success. You probably don't intend to be careless with the more fragile hearts around you, but there is a good chance that you are and you don't even know it. I have been guilty of this in my lifetime, and it grieves me to think of how I have added to burdens with my harshness and pride. I have bruised many reeds and blown out many flickering torches, at least humanly speaking. I thank God that he has not given me the power to ruin anyone, or I would surely be guilty of this crime. I am not very strong, but I am stronger than some and have wielded that strength in crushing ways. I praise God that his grace is still sufficient for all my sins.

Are you a crushing strong person? Is there a wake of wounded souls behind you—people you blame for being oversensitive, people you despise or ignore for being weak? Think carefully about your strength and where it came from. Did you grow up in a home full of grace and health? That was God's gift to you, for you had no choice over the family that would raise you. Although the shaping influences of our young lives are in no way determinative of our futures, God has ordained that they do have a strong influence on the kinds of problems we will face during our lifetime. Have you grown up in difficult circumstances and overcome many adversities, so that you expect others to step up to the plate and do the same? If so, you may have forgotten who gave you the desire and ability to overcome those obstacles. No matter how you slice it, your strength is not your own, and if you think it is, you just might inflict a great deal of misery on others with your expectations that they be strong like you.

If you suspect that this might describe you, do not despair. Sadly, it describes many Christians, some of them pastors and leaders in our churches. Yet God's grace is sufficient for you. In every situation where you have destroyed and damaged, Jesus has nurtured and cared patiently for others in your place. Notice his gentleness with weak faith in the boat with his disciples. Think about his love for the sinful woman in Luke chapter 7. His obedience stands in your place as well, and his wounds plead for you before the Father. Ask him to open your eyes and humble you, and then celebrate his outrageous love for bullies and fearful people alike.

Though your sins are like a mountain, his righteousness soars above them all and reaches the throne of grace to disarm the wrath of God and merit for you the eternal delight of your heavenly Father. Praise God, we are not under law, but always bathed in the gushing fountain of his amazing grace!

FOR FURTHER REFLECTION

1. Do you tend to feel proud when you stand strong as a Christian? Would it disappoint you to discover that your obedience isn't really yours at all? Why?

2. In what ways might it be great news that, even as a Christian, you can't generate obedience to God without his active intervention to give you the desire and ability to obey? Why are you not free to stop trying to obey God? What do you think it might look like to keep trying to obey God with the knowledge that you don't possess the power to obey him in yourself?

3. What sins in your life have seemed easy to overcome? Have you ever wondered why others can't just stop sinning like you did? What sins have defeated you in spite of your biggest efforts to change? Why?

4. As you consider yourself with sober judgment, what kind of faith has God granted you so far? What gifts has he given you? How much grace to change is he giving you at the moment?

5. Since we tend to be profoundly blind to ourselves, what kind of help should we seek as we try to evaluate those things?

6. How does Scripture encourage us to behave toward other believers who struggle with doubt and fear?

7. In what ways have you wounded people around you with your strength? What truths will help you to survive recognizing your own failure in this area?

CHAPTER TEN

suffering sinners

A man, truly illuminated, will no more despise others,
than Bartimeus, after his own eyes were opened, would
take a stick, and beat every blind man he met.
—John Newton[1]

Sin almost always makes us miserable. Oh, it may seem like a good idea at the time, and it promises all sorts of fun and delight, but in the end sin always complicates our lives, hurts ourselves and others, and leaves us guilty, ashamed, and feeling cut off from the love of God. In the book of Proverbs, we learn that the twisted way of the transgressor is full of thorns and snares (Prov. 22:5). That matches our own life experience. We suffer intensely from the bitter fruit of our own stupidity, foolish appetites, disordered desires, and over-desires for good things.

Many of us, however, find it difficult to respond to our own sin and that of others with pity and compassion. We think that if we fail to be tough on sin or if we celebrate too much how God has been tough on sin by punishing Christ in our place, then we are condoning and enabling sin in ourselves and others. As a result, our posture is often one of exasperation and judgment toward repeat offenders, rather than one of loving compassion and understanding. We may be patient with the addict so long as he is trying hard to recover. We might respond with grace when he falls the first few times, but love and tenderness quickly run out in the face of relentless failure.

Yet when Jesus interacted with serious sinners—some of whom were also serial sinners—his posture was always one of gentleness and encouragement. He called sin what it is and never excused it, yet at the same time he never crushed anyone with the truth or rubbed their noses in their failure. He had plenty of abrasive and caustic words for the self-righteous Pharisees, but the broken repeat offender found a gentle and forgiving welcome in him.

JIM'S STORY

If John Newton's depiction of the Christian life is true and accurate to Scripture, then we have great reason to have loving compassion toward others when they are caught up in patterns of sin from which they cannot break free. If they are completely dependent on the specific and powerful grace of God to see their sin clearly and repent from it, then there may be long periods of time when they know they should repent yet are unable to do so.

That's what happened to Jim. A lovable and hospitable man who was well versed in the Bible and theology, he was an elder at a church where my husband was serving as an interim pastor. We enjoyed many lunches and delightful conversations about the Lord in his home, and we never dreamed that he would fall from grace so drastically. Jim did not consider himself a good-looking man, and therefore he reckoned it safe to counsel a few of the women in his church. He reasoned that no woman would find him attractive since he was overweight and average in the looks department. He was wrong. He began to counsel a beautiful woman who was married to an irresponsible, alcoholic husband, and she found many things attractive about this religious man who worked hard to provide for his family. It wasn't long before Jim and Valerie became emotionally and sexually involved with one another. By the time my husband was informed of these things, Valerie was pregnant with Jim's child and two families were destroyed.

Sin seemed like a lot of fun for a while. Jim and Valerie were infatuated with each other and completely caught up in their new life together. They left their spouses and seemed untroubled by the devastating impact this had on the seven young children whose lives and homes were shattered. My husband, along with the other elders of the church, pleaded with Jim and worked hard to reason with him, but it was no use. He agreed with them that what he was doing was wrong, but he was captivated by Valerie and unshakable in his determination to have her. So, after being granted a reasonable time for repentance, Jim was excommunicated from his church—not for committing this sin, but for his failure to repent. We were all saddened by this horribly painful turn of events.

As life settled back down and we all struggled to live with this new reality, we wondered what to do with Jim. He had a lot of theological knowledge, and in the following months he found himself with a reality that surprised him. He knew that the church had done the right thing in excommunicating him, but it irritated him a lot. He knew that what he had done and was doing was wrong and sinful, yet his heart remained stony and hard. He asked if he could come to visit us, and we agreed to meet with him again, though we wondered what we could ever say or do to make a difference. We were also strongly tempted to be angry with him. We saw the devastation that his actions had caused and wondered how a man could be so selfish as to devastate his own children in the pursuit of his new love. He was completely blind to their pain and full of reasons why his actions made sense.

Newton's teachings helped us to love Jim in his blindness. We realized that since we are all dependent on the Holy Spirit for eyes to see our sin, and only he can give us soft and repentant hearts, God might leave Jim in this place for a long time. I vividly remember the day when Jim sat in our living room and said, "I know that I should be sorry for all of this and that I should repent, but I can't. I'm glad I did this and I would do it all over again." We reminded Jim that he should repent, but that he couldn't possibly do it without God's help. As 2 Timothy 2:25 shows us, repentance is a gift that God grants, not something we can work up within ourselves. We told Jim that we loved him and would not stop praying that God would move in his heart and give him the sweet gift of repentance.

We didn't hear from Jim for almost two years, but finally the call came. God had been faithful, and because of his great love for two big sinners, God had melted two hearts with repentance. Jim and his new wife were flooded with awe, wonder, joy, and gratitude that he would extend his love and forgiveness to such blind and willful people as them. Jim could not stop praising God, and his joy drove him to want to make things as right as he could in light of all that had happened. When God finally opened his eyes and showed Jim the magnitude of his sin and the devastating impact it had on so many lives, he was almost undone. Yet something else was also at work in and through his sin. Jim began to build two Ebenezers in his life. One was a memorial to the towering skyscraper of his atrocious and destructive sin. The other, right next to it, was a beautiful, breathtaking shrine to commemorate the outrageous love of the God who, instead of destroying him for his sin, chose to hang on a cross and pay for that sin in order to win him back. Jim went back to his old church and made a full confession before the congregation. He was restored to fellowship and to the Lord's Table, and he is still singing God's praises and telling everyone that, though he was and continues to be a big sinner, he has a much bigger Savior.

I would like to believe that I could never do what Jim and Valerie did, but of course I can and, given half a chance, I will. If David, the anointed King of Israel, the man after God's own heart, could commit adultery and murder, then surely I could do this too, should God leave me to myself for a moment and give me the opportunity. The more God helps me to believe this, the more able I am to love high-handed sinners and feel compassion for all the misery that their sin brings. Jim and Valerie will spend the rest of their lives living with the effects of their sin on their children. God's grace will be sufficient for this, and he will use their sin for the good of their children too, but it will not be easy. They will know grief and regret at the same time as they rejoice in God's faithfulness to them. They will have many opportunities to hate their sin, yet love what God did in their hearts through it.

Before he fell, Jim was a proud and self-righteous man who knew his doctrine well but found it difficult to love others and bear with those whose doctrine was flawed. He was a spectator to grace; he admired the concept and enjoyed talking about its theological implications, but felt no deep personal need of it himself. He is a different man today, a joyful recipient of the grace he once only admired from a distance. As a result, he now daily exercises a ministry of compassionate counsel to the workers and clients outside an abortion clinic. The way of the transgressor is hard and humbling indeed, yet full of remarkable sweetness and joy for those whom God calls to repentance.

PATIENCE WITH OUR OWN SIN

Understanding how God works in the lives of his children not only helps us to know how to love others, it also teaches us how to view ourselves more accurately when we are locked into patterns of sin that we know we should put off but cannot bring ourselves to shed. God is up to something good even through our worst sins—in fact, especially through our worst sins. When we understand and experience our own profound inability to obey or repent, we may become more patient and tender people who at last see the beams in our own eyes more clearly than we see the specks in others' (Matt. 7:3–4). Our sin may fashion us into people who lovingly call others to repentance without a spirit of superiority and judgment, but with tremendous love and gentleness (Gal. 6:1).

There are many areas of my life in which I would like to change and have asked God to change me, but I haven't yet grown. For example, I struggle to be a loving pastor's wife toward the women in our church. I have a dear friend who is the kind of pastor's wife I wish I could be. She is so lovingly interested in the lives of the people in her church, and she serves them and cares for them patiently. She remembers all their birthdays and the important and not-so-important details of their lives and the lives of their children. She plans strategically to host people in her home for a meal, and she fellowships faithfully with the women in her church through Bible studies and social events. That's the kind of pastor's wife I would like to be, but God has not chosen to make me into the soft sweetie pie I would like to be who gushes love to everyone around me.

Instead, I am prone to valuing people based on what they do or don't do for the church (and in a church plant there is always plenty to be done!). I affirm people who I value, but I am equally prone to judging and disliking people strongly and to having a heart that flares easily if I think people have unfair expectations of me. Right now there is someone in my life who I should forgive for a rather serious offense, and I don't want to forgive her. In fact, I can barely look at her. I know that I have no grounds whatsoever upon which to hold this grudge. I should forgive her as freely as I have been forgiven, but I don't want to. What am I to make of myself? In a sense, this coldness in my heart runs contradictory to every single thing I have written in this book about the wonders of the gospel. Still I find that I can't melt my own heart or even drum up the desire for it to be melted.

I am stuck, but at the same time I can be at peace for now with my inability to do as I should. I understand that I will never be able to want to forgive without an act of God on my heart. Indeed, in another sense, everything I feel in my heart right now simply verifies all that I have learned. There is no switch that I can flip to make myself want to love this lady, no spiritual discipline I can perform to bring my unruly heart into line. As I wrestle unsuccessfully with my heart, Satan mocks me with the gospel on a regular basis, saying, "How dare you teach others about God's grace and forgiveness when you can't even look at this lady without despising her!" He's right, of course; *I* have no right to open my mouth at all, but the gospel isn't about me to begin with. Instead it is about the incredible grace of God that has appeared in Jesus—good news that is now declared through flawed messengers who desperately need the same grace about which we speak to others.

So in the same way that I can have compassion on others when their sin makes their lives desperately hard, and can trust that God will certainly use their sin that he hates to accomplish good things that he loves in their lives, I can have compassion on myself—trusting God to use my own sin for his glory and my good too. After all, even now Jesus looks at my sin-stained and unforgiving heart and declares "no condemnation" (Rom. 8:1). Ought I not to agree with his assessment of my status before God, rather than Satan's?

PATIENCE WITH THE SIN OF OTHERS

In his writings, John Newton expressed tremendous compassion with weak, repetitive sinners. He reasons like this:

A company of travelers fall into a pit: one of them gets a passenger to draw him out. Now he should not be angry with the
rest for falling in; nor because they are not yet out, as he is.
He did not pull himself out: instead, therefore, of reproaching
them, he should show them pity. . . . A man, truly illuminated,
will no more despise others, than Bartimeus, after his own
eyes were opened, would take a stick, and beat every blind
man he met.[2]

William Cowper, the poet and hymn writer, was origi-
nally trained to be a lawyer but had to give up that ambition
because of his depression. He attempted suicide three times
and was institutionalized for a while in an asylum for severe
depression. It was there in the asylum that he came to faith
in Christ, through the influence of an evangelical doctor.
Cowper began attending Newton's church when he moved to
Olney, and he and Newton became close friends, collaborating
on hymn-writing projects. Yet his struggles with depression
returned, to the point where he was no longer even able to
attend church. Newton continued to care for and encourage
Cowper, taking long walks with him and helping him in the
midst of black despair.[3]

What a wonderful providence of God that he led these two
men to be richly blessed by one another. Newton saw God's glory
in Cowper, and with great gentleness and patience sought to
relieve his suffering and make his gifts available to the body of
Christ. He did not rebuke Cowper for his weak faith or ongoing struggle with depression, but he walked with him lovingly.
Though never cured, Cowper experienced a remission of his
depression for a period of about nine years, which coincided
with his discovery of the doctrines of grace. These relieved his
conscience and persuaded him, in his best moments, that his
safety rested in God's grip on him and not on the strength of
his own faith. Newton's understanding of the suffering that sin

and weakness cause made him a man full of mercy and grace toward those who remained unable to thrive emotionally under the burdens God called them to bear.

Newton's own careful analysis of the state of the believer caused him, like the mature Christian he described in his letters, to make every allowance for other believers' failure.[4] His response to those who wrote to him in a state of despair over their ongoing sin never held the tone of "How could you do that?" Rather, his response was habitually "Of course you did that: you're a sinner, and that's what sinners do."[5] He reasoned that sinners have so many things going against them in this world that we should never be shocked when they fall. Instead, we should be constantly amazed when they don't!

The first of these huge obstacles that stand between believers and holy lives is the powerful reality of our remaining depravity. It is a sad and heavy thing to know the gospel, to experience the powerful and incredible grace of God, and yet to sin and want to sin against it. It's bad enough to sin against the law of God, but so much worse to sin against him in the face of his outrageous love and sacrificial provision for all of our sin.[6] Yet this we do, time and time again.

I am reminded of the time when our second son, Sam, held the power to disrupt my peace and joy. He was a delightful baby—at least until he started sitting in a high chair to eat his meals. This was an adventure for him, but he quickly began to delight in playing with his food. Sometimes he would put his food on his head, while at other times he would throw it as far as he could. I knew we couldn't let this bad habit develop into a lifestyle, so I determined to nip it in the bud right away. I said, "Sam, NO! You may not do that. Mommy will have to spank you if you do that again." This speech had no impact whatsoever; he looked me coyly in the eye and did it again. This time I had to follow through with my threat, so I took that tiny little hand

and spanked it once, then warned him again. This audacious little cherub barely cried, looked me in the eye, and repeated his actions.

The battle continued. Soon, after flinging his food, he held his hand up to me to be spanked while he cringed and waited for the smack. Such was his commitment to incredible rebellion! He didn't stop to think for a minute about our loving provision for him in giving him his food or dressing him or loving him comprehensively; he was just determined to win the battle. By God's grace, Sam did finally give up the battle and has grown into a joyful, engaging young Christian man who loves the Lord. God was merciful to him and to us by persuading him that this kind of rebellion really wasn't worth the effort! However, for a few months there, it seemed that his perseverance might defeat us!

What a blessing to know that our stubborn attachment to sin can never defeat the love of God for his children! Like my little boy, we seem to reach deeper and deeper levels of ugliness when we persevere in our sin despite the oceans of God's grace gushing in our direction daily. We really are that bad, and when God opens our eyes to see the depths of this kind of rebellion it is a difficult thing to survive. It is no surprise that so many believers live in shame and depression in the face of such revelations, particularly if the system of doctrine they hold to does not prepare them for the truth that this is how it is meant to be. God planned it all this way so that we would come to see our great need for him and treasure all he has done for us, discovering that no matter how evil we may truly be, his grace is greater still.[7] This comforting truth is rarely heard.

Furthermore, Christians have a very powerful adversary. Satan is old and experienced at his craft. He has been tempting people for centuries, and he delights in his skill and the power God allows him to exert over those he cannot ultimately defeat. It is interesting to explore the characteristic sins we struggle with and to see how effective Satan is at drawing us into a cascade of thoughts that ultimately leads to sin. We can even step back and evaluate this, diagnosing it and teasing it apart, yet get sucked right back into it the next moment and flounder helplessly toward its inevitable conclusion. It is ridiculous, yet powerful and gripping all at once.

Satan knows the shaping influences of our lives and the habitual patterns we fall into, and he makes the most of it. I told you of my great struggle with food. You might think that since I am no longer obese I have mastered some self-control in this area. Yet I find myself drawn once again into a powerful struggle with this old and abiding enemy. I am at this moment locked into mortal combat with McDonald's chicken nuggets. Until two months ago, I hadn't eaten a chicken nugget in thirty years and was never even tempted to do so. However, while I waited at an automotive shop for my car to be repaired recently, I ended up watching a television show in which two cardiologists were asked to find the tastiest and healthiest choices from fast food restaurants. One of them sang the praises of these crispy delights. Ever since then, I can't seem to stop myself from pulling into the drive-through and indulging in these tempting treasures, with barbecue and sweet and sour sauce, of course.

This is both funny and sad all at once. God is currently turning me over to something that I never dreamed I would struggle with, and Satan is an expert at drawing me into the thought pattern that makes this sound like the best idea in the whole world . . . until I've finished all ten pieces and don't feel so well anymore. On my own I am absolutely no match for Satan's power to draw me into sinful thinking, so of course I sin unless I am rescued.

Finally, we live in a world so full of temptation and opportunity that it is a wonder we grow in obedience at all. I counsel many young men and women who are addicted to pornography and who feel deep shame over this sin. Even those who struggle with pride, greed, and self-righteousness without much guilt usually feel a great deal of shame over this sexual sin and go to great lengths to reform. However, it is a struggle that is particularly resistant to efforts to change. The powerful addictive nature of all the feel–good chemicals that are released in the process of looking at porn and masturbating makes it tough to overcome. The combination of shame and the inability to stop usually gets a person's attention.

When has porn ever been so easy to get as it is now, with the advent of the Internet? You used to have to risk something to get it when it was sold in shops, but now you can indulge in private and leave no trace behind. When a young person is shredded with this battle and comes for help, they expect to hear a pastor or counselor say something in the line of "How could you?", when what they should hear is "How could you not?" We live in a highly sexualized society with visual and audible messages assaulting us at every turn. We have bodies that are wired for the pleasure of sex. And in the case of college students, who are often delaying marriage for the sake of pursuing careers, the battle is intense against very normal hormones and desires. We put ourselves and others into a position ripe for failure and then we act surprised when people fail.

A mature believer studies all the aspects of a person's struggle with sin and makes many allowances. He never stops calling sin the ugly and evil thing that it is, but he understands how deeply rooted it is in our human nature and how helpless every Christian is to stand against it. This, together with his profound understanding of his own heart, makes him soft and tender toward sinning Christians and able to encourage and restore with compassion and humility. This realistic expectation of himself and others, combined with a strong and glorious view of the excellency of the gospel, fashions a steadiness in the soul that is not shaken by the worst that men and Satan can do. Sin should not shock us or surprise us when we discover it in ourselves and others. We should expect it.

SO WHAT?

I have had the great joy and privilege of watching truth change people. It is inevitable. God is at work in the lives of his people, and since most of my ministry has been to women in the church, I get to watch women grow. When I teach this material to a new group of women, something begins to happen automatically. We may never address marriage directly, but marriages begin to change. Once someone becomes a recipient of grace, it begins to flow out of them toward others and it is priceless to watch. As we get to the third and fourth studies, ladies begin piping up and saying, "You know, as I'm starting to understand how unable I am to change myself, I see that my husband is also in this same predicament. No matter how hard I nag him, he can't just get his act together and change any more than I can." They start nagging less and praying more. In fact, when you really come to believe that we are helpless and dependent on God for all change, you start praying a lot more, not because you think you should, but because you want to. You see that it is the only way to real transformation.

Humility changes our relationships a great deal. Understanding weakness changes the way we parent our children as well. It is so tempting to lecture our young ones and tell them how they should think, feel, and act. It is not so easy to come alongside them as a co-sinner and talk to them about how impossible obedience is. We may be able to force outward obedience upon them, but we are powerless to change their hearts. We can't make ourselves repentant, sorry, or tenderhearted, but somehow we feel justified in demanding these things of them. We shame them until they cave under pressure and learn to perform for our pleasure, but the long-term results of that approach are never pretty. So many Christian children grow up and leave home completely unprepared to see and wrestle with their own sinful hearts because they've never had a chance to see and confess the truth of their own weakness. They are taught to trust and obey and march like a soldier in God's conquering army, until it all disintegrates and they fall into sins they never thought a Christian could possibly commit.

Likewise, many parents are afraid to admit their own weakness to their children for fear that it will give their kids a license to sin. So we lock everyone into an impossible situation. In reality, of course, our children can see us sin! They watch us all the time. If we do not confess our sin openly and explain it to them, we risk losing all credibility before them.

It might feel scary to trust the Holy Spirit with our children's spiritual development, but he is far more able and willing to grow them spiritually than we could ever be. If you worry that telling children how unable they are to obey without God's help will give them an excuse to keep sinning, perhaps you should give it a try and see how it works out. In the times when you must demand outward obedience of them, explain to them that they can't possibly change their own hearts. Instead of immediately punishing their anger, enter into it and understand it. Of course they feel helpless, rebellious, and angry. Their will is being crossed. Explain to them how often you feel anger too. They could probably tell you all about it anyway. Show them how helpless your own heart is and what you both need to do with hearts like that.

Explain to your children what they truly need. They need God to soften their hearts and make them want to obey, and they need him to give them the strength to obey. Then celebrate with them everything they have in Christ. Their sins have been paid for by the blood of Christ, and they are covered by his obedient goodness like a glowing robe surrounding them. Celebrate Christ, pray for them, and expect God to do his work through the Holy Spirit over the course of time. Understanding your own inability will help you to help them learn to deal with the reality of their fallen hearts and to cherish the breathtaking good news of the gospel. It will help you to feel more compassion and understanding and less frustration and irritation. After all, they are sinners just like you.

Compassion and humility will also lead us sometimes voluntarily to allow others to sin against us. There are times, of course, when this is not the right approach. A woman who is being beaten by her husband should not volunteer to take that abuse and let him sin against her in this way. She needs to protect herself and help her husband by clearing out of harm's way and finding help for both of them. However, there are times when it is a godly thing to volunteer to let others sin against you, to stand in the gap and bear the pain of allowing others to treat you badly. I don't know about you, but when I am sinned against there is a roar that rises in my heart to shout, "How dare you treat me that way!" It is the hardest thing in the world for me to allow others to treat me with disrespect and disregard.

Yet Jesus volunteered for just that kind of treatment. His love covered a multitude of sins, both in terms of those he died for and in the cases of those he interacted with here on earth. He never demanded to be treated as he deserved, and in the end he volunteered to be beaten, abused, hated, and despised in order to rescue his people. We are invited to become like that.

Recently, when I felt righteous indignation rising within me and the words "How dare you?" reverberated in my head, I was rescued by the precious thought that, actually, I was the one who dared. I am the one who has dared to trample on the Son of God and treat him as though he were irrelevant or a mean taskmaster. I often dare to accuse him of not caring, and I often dare to complain about his will. Why on earth does he tolerate such ridiculous and outrageous rebellion from me? He tolerates it because he has already paid the price for it all, and he is committed to my spiritual growth and blessing.

The more I see myself as the biggest sinner and the worst transgressor, the more I will be able to step up to love others even when they sin against me time and time again. These are precious moments when I get a tiny glimpse of what it must have felt like to be Jesus. I can't imagine what it was like for the sinless Son of God, the Creator of all things, to hang on a cross helplessly while the creatures he made mocked and murdered him. He could have shaken himself free at any moment with a cosmic "How dare you?" that would have destroyed them forever and vindicated him in all his glory and righteousness. But in love, he volunteered to stay on the cross and suffer the indignity, humiliation, and pain of accepting the mockery of beings so inferior to him that it is mind-melting.

Yet when I volunteer to let others treat me badly out of love, I get to participate in that suffering for just a moment. As I do so, I am once again filled with awe and wonder that Jesus Christ would set his love upon me for his own good pleasure and choose to suffer and die for me. As Charles Wesley put it, "Amazing love, how can it be, that thou my God shouldst die for me?"[8]

WHAT ABOUT YOU?

Are you afraid that having compassion on yourself for your sin struggles will lead you into more and more sin? That is not my experience as a Christian, a mother, or a biblical counselor. What happens when people become anxious, depressed, and discouraged over their sin? They start feeling really bad, and that sensation drives them to seek relief from dreadful feelings. I have counseled people who turned to food, alcohol, porn, prostitutes, overachieving, good grades, approval of parents, cutting, cleaning, organizing, Bible reading, and fasting and prayer. There are many behaviors, good and bad, that we can turn to in order to drown out the drumbeat of perpetual personal failure. The bad behaviors bring pleasure for a minute and then plunge the sufferer even more deeply into shame and distress, thus perpetuating the cycle. The good behaviors comfort for a minute with a likeness of spiritual goodness, but they soon disappoint because they don't last. God loves us too much to let us find lasting peace in any behavior, even the good ones. We can be hard on ourselves in a way that God is not, and we castigate and punish ourselves in ungodly ways for our ungodliness.

God is very patient with us and always remembers that we are weak people made of dust. We don't want to be weak and dusty people, so we fight that truth by insisting that we are strong when we're not. God is glorified in our weakness in so many ways. How would we ever know his patience if we did not sin time and time again? How could we ever plumb the depths of his love if we did not sin against it over and over again, only to find that his forgiveness is endless and his love unshakable? As Newton would put it,

> Well, when we have said all we can of the abounding of sin in us—grace still *more* abounds in Jesus. We cannot be so evil as he is good. His power is a good match for our weakness. His riches are a good match for our poverty. His mercy is a good match for our misery. We are vile in ourselves—but we are complete in him. In ourselves we have cause to be abased—but in him we may rejoice. Blessed be God for Jesus Christ![9]

It is possible to hate your sin and at the same time be compassionate toward your own weakness. Sometimes we act as though there are only two options: either we hate our sin and punish ourselves for it, or we give ourselves a break, which leads toward careless and escalating amounts of sin. There is another way. Like the apostle Paul, we can hate our sin and plan not to do it, yet understand our weakness and accept it, casting ourselves on the mercy of God. Paul is right when he exclaims, "Wretched man that I am!" (Rom. 7:24). We are all wretched sinners throughout our lifetimes. Paul does not chase this thought away with a better plan to read the Bible and pray more. He cries out, "Who will deliver me from this body of death? Thanks be to God through Christ Jesus our Lord!" (Rom. 7:24–25). He has already been delivered by the death of Christ, and he knows that he will be delivered comprehensively and forever in the life to come.

Paul doesn't seem to worry that his declaration of his own struggle with sin will encourage us all to sin more. He knows that he is weak, and he has told us this time and time again and even dared to boast in his weakness. Paul does not seem to be tied up in knots about his ongoing sin problem, but he moves seamlessly and immediately to doxology. It is dazzling. Paul does not spend hours, days, months, and years agonizing over his sin, as we so often do. This kind of morbid misery doesn't help us sin less; it simply leads to more and more cycles of sin.

Take my current struggle to forgive another weak sinner who I know I should love and care for. There is a proper and healthy way in which I should feel shame for this. I have drunk deeply at the fountain of grace, so how dare I refuse to show similar grace to another? And yet I find myself doing this very thing. I could be undone by my sin, and in the process add to it a host of others. Sometimes my sin even makes me want to insist that my husband leave the ministry. "Since I can't do this well," I reason, "it would be better not to do this at all." Sometimes I eat to anesthetize myself from the guilt that I feel, or I make excuses and blame others, or I take out my anger on my children. Despair over my sin frequently acts as the gateway to many, many more sins, not fewer.

Now imagine what might happen if, like Paul, I were to run to the cross right away. Suppose in the midst of my sin I were to fall on my face before my merciful Father, to confess my sin in all its depth and ugliness, owning up that this sin truly is an accurate measure of my heart's sickness and depravity, while asking for the abundant grace that I need in that moment. In that case, while I myself am more and more abased over my sin, at the same time I will be learning how to rejoice in the finished work of Christ in my place while prancing in the festival robes of the righteousness that Christ earned for me and that are freely given to me by faith. This is how despair turns into joy and cycles of sin are gradually cut off at their root.

DYNAMIC DUET

Worship and heart introspection can be a powerful team. If we become competent at understanding and celebrating our union with Christ in a way that leads to joy, but never take the time or have the courage to examine our hearts, then we get stuck. We enjoy our salvation greatly, perhaps, but don't get the privilege of watching God dismantle the idolatries of our hearts and lead us on to deeper and purer worship. On the other hand, if we only examine our hearts without learning to rejoice and celebrate the imputed righteousness of Christ, we are in danger of a morbid type of introspection that robs us of the joy we are meant to experience in our Savior. However, when God enables us to connect deeply with the truth of how he loves us just as we are, even when we can't change, our responding joy in worship can be the fuel that propels us onward to do the hard and potentially discouraging work of taking a good long look at our hearts and coming up with creative ways to try to change.

The good news of the gospel is precisely what gives us the courage to be honest about our sin without being undone by it. It is possible and delightful to engage in soul searching when you are confident that God is not ashamed of you and will never abandon you, no matter what sins you find lurking there. Confession becomes a relief, while repentance is possible only when we know what it is that we need to repent of. When we grasp the gospel we do not need to be afraid of what we will find in our hearts, for God's grace is far greater than all our sin.

FOR FURTHER REFLECTION

1. In what ways do you tend to suffer from your own sin? Do you tend to judge yourself harshly for your sin, or to look on yourself with pity?

2. Has there ever been a time in your life when you knew you should repent but couldn't? What was that like? What did you do?

3. How would your feelings and actions differ if you believed that repentance is a gift from God?

4. What does it mean to sin against God's law? What does it mean to sin against his love? In what ways do you still do that?

5. In what characteristic ways do you tend to sin repeatedly? How does your own sinful flesh lead you into sin? In what ways is Satan proficient at luring you into sin? In what ways do worldly things draw you into sin?

6. How do you feel after you sin? How do you tend to deal with that feeling?

7. How would life be different for you if you did not feel anxious or depressed over the fact that you continue to sin, but could move directly to worship?

CHAPTER ELEVEN

unbearable love

*The repeated and multiplied pardons which he has
received, increase his admiration of, and the sense of
his obligations to, the rich sovereign abounding mercy
of the covenant.* —John Newton[1]

I had been dreading this moment for a several months. I
knew I had to tell him the truth, but the words simply
would not come out of my mouth. So, instead of saying
what I needed to say, I found other ways to fill the awkward
and painful silence. "Well, I've never taken illegal drugs or
stolen anything of value . . ."

"That's good!" he said patiently, waiting for me to divulge
the important piece of information I had said I must tell him.

I couldn't look at him as I continued to squirm. "I've never
been drunk . . . well, maybe once, but never again!"

He didn't respond immediately this time, but let my words
hang in the air for a moment. Then he put his arm around me
and said, "I think I know what you're trying to tell me."

We'd finally arrived at the moment of truth that I was sure
would ruin everything. "You do?" I asked, as tears filled my eyes
and fear gripped my heart. "And . . . what do you think of me
now?" I asked.

He said, "I think if I'd had the opportunity, I would have done the very same thing. The only difference between you and me is that God didn't let me have the opportunity." They were simple words, really, and yet with those few words he changed my life forever.

MY DOUBLE LIFE

The truth was that for many years I had lived a double life. I started dating a young man when I was fourteen years old, and for the first six years of that relationship we had been paragons of virtue and propriety. I was proud of many things, but proudest of our chastity and determination not to descend into sexual sin, despite many opportunities and a heart increasingly given to fantasy and lust. It wasn't easy, but we were doing pretty well—at least until I found stacks and stacks of pornography in his bedroom one day.

I should have confronted him lovingly and helped him to find good counsel, but that's not what I did. Instead, I looked at those magazines and chose to plunge myself into a world of deceit and gratification. I deceived myself in many ways, convincing myself that his problem was my fault because I was frustrating him with my determination to remain a virgin until we married. My wicked and sinful heart craved him, and it now became clear that I would do anything to hold onto him. I was also sure that if he didn't marry me, no one ever would. I believed it would be better to be married to a loser than to be single forever. I told myself that God would be pleased for us to sleep together, so long as we actually did get married eventually. I told myself a lot of lies, and I convinced myself that those lies were coming from God himself. Lying became easy and natural throughout the next four years.

At that time I was a leader in my campus Christian ministry and heading up our small group Bible studies. I lied to my friends and ministry leaders. I deceived my parents and lied to my pastor who expressed concern over my relationship with my boyfriend. I allowed people to believe that I was pure and chaste when I was anything and everything but that. As the years progressed, it became evident to me that this boyfriend was not a good candidate for husband and father to my children, but now I had to make it all right. Having slept with him, I believed I could make it up to God and everyone else by staying with him until we married. It was the only way I thought I could deal with the crippling guilt of so much sin.

Notice how tied up I was in the silliness of my own mind! I never asked for help; I never sought advice and godly counsel. I was far too proud to let anyone know that I had committed what I thought was the worst sin ever, and I was determined to atone for it myself and make it right with God. As the relationship began to falter and fall apart, I became more and more desperate. I had just graduated from college and had been asked to consider serving as a short-term missionary in a hospital laboratory in Liberia, West Africa. I thought maybe that would help me to atone for my sin, as well as being fun for a while.

There has probably never been a more confused and improperly motivated missionary in the history of the world than I was at the age of twenty-one. Tormented by guilt and fear that I would never marry, I marched through all of the required challenges to be accepted as a missionary, carefully editing my story to suit my audience. I left for Liberia with a half-hearted pledge of marriage from my boyfriend, who was finishing college, and a promise ring on my finger. I was a walking, living, breathing lie.

An interesting thing happened when I got to Africa. I met up with a young woman who had attended the same church where my boyfriend and I had met. She had heard all about us, and none of it was good. She knew that my family did not approve of my fiancé; in fact, no one who knew and loved me approved of this relationship. In love, and with great determination, she would not stop talking to me about it. I reluctantly shared a glimpse of the truth with her, and she graciously informed me that I was under no spiritual obligation to marry him and that I must break up with him instead. "But I love him!" I sobbed. "So what?" she responded. "Love is easy, and you can love anyone. But you do not respect him, and you must not marry a man you can't respect."

There it was: the sentence that by God's grace pierced my hard heart and accomplished what years of pleading from my parents and many others never had. Two days later I wrote the letter that ended ten years of strife and rebellion, but also shattered all my hopes and dreams of marriage and motherhood. I was absolutely sure that I would be single forever now. What godly man would ever want me after all those years of sinning and covering up?

UNDESERVED GRACE

Three months later, Iain arrived on our compound from the UK to work as an electrical engineer. Our friendship had gotten off to a rough start over the cultural differences between the British and Americans, but one year later I found myself deeply in love with a man I greatly respected. Somehow I now sat next to this godly man, and his words of compassion, humility, grace, and kindness were like a bombshell to my soul! I expected disgust. I expected rebuke and rejection. Instead I was welcomed into forgiveness, and I could hardly bear it. I knew what I deserved! I deserved to be trapped in a miserable marriage with a man who I didn't respect or love anymore and to be stuck there for the rest of my life. Instead it seemed that God was offering me the best of the best, the cream of the crop, a prince among men! This was not how things were supposed to work out. Doesn't the Bible tell us that we reap what we sow (Gal. 6:7)? Don't we get what we deserve? So how could this be? God seemed to be giving me the polar opposite of what I deserved, and I was seriously confused.

On that day the ground seemed to shift beneath my feet as old strongholds of self-righteousness began to crumble. This was the day I began to understand the gospel. I had always believed that I was saved through faith in Christ alone, but in the classic style of a baby Christian I had turned that into a bargain with God. The deal was that if I gave him faith and obedience, he would give me salvation, blessing, and his favor. In the words of the classic hymn, I believed that if I trusted and obeyed, then God owed me happiness in Jesus. If I didn't do my part, though, I was pretty much on my own. I didn't yet know that even my faith to trust was his gift to me, or that I would have to depend on him for every single moment of obedience throughout my whole life. I surely hadn't held up my end of the deal, so I was sure that God would pounce at some point and make me pay for all these sins.

It is important to add the observation that if God had allowed me to reap the earthly consequences of all my sin at this point, he would still have been completely good and justified. God doesn't always rescue us from the consequences of our sins. Although he has once and for all removed the eternal punishment that my sin deserves by placing it on Christ, he often leaves me to suffer the bitter aftereffects of my sin and mistakes here on earth in order to humble me, teach me dependence, and train me in righteousness.[2]

There are general principles in Scripture that apply throughout life. It is certainly true that in general we do reap what we sow; if we work hard we reap prosperity, while if we are lazy we will be hungry. However, there are moments in the lives of most believers when God executes a grand reversal, as if his intention were to take your breath away and show you the depth of his heart of kindness. There are the terrifying times when we know we have blown it so badly that surely God must expose and punish us for our own good. And then something completely different happens. God not only withholds the punishment we so richly deserve, but he lavishes us with loving-kindness and surprises us with joy.

John Newton experienced that surprising kindness of God many times in his life. During one period in his life he spent a desperately miserable year in West Africa, where he was a virtual slave of his employer. He had arrived at this sorry state through years of immaturity and flagrant rebellion against God and those with authority over him during this seafaring journey. At one point he fell sick and nearly died; at others he was virtually starving to death. At length a ship came with instructions to look for him and providentially arrived exactly where he was working. Had the ship arrived a few days later, he would have been inland on a trading trip. Had it arrived much earlier, he would have been working at a factory elsewhere.

On the journey home, the ship almost sank several times—in fact, had it not been carrying a cargo of beeswax and wood, both of which are lighter than water, it would certainly have gone down. At one point during the storm, the captain sent him below to fetch a knife, and the man who took Newton's place was immediately swept overboard to his death. All these remarkable deliverances took place while he was still an angry blasphemer against God. We don't always get what we deserve in this life; in fact, sometimes we get the exact opposite.[3]

DAVID'S STORY

King David knew exactly what this kind of unbearable and utterly undeserved love felt like. There were many times in his life when he experienced the love and protection of God, which we can read about in the psalms he left for us. There is another story in David's life, however, when God blessed him richly in spite of his willful sin and rebellion. David desperately wanted to build a temple for the Lord (2 Sam. 7). After all, that is what successful kings were supposed to do in the ancient world, and who better to do it than *this* particular king, the man after God's own heart? After all, God had given him rest from his enemies all around, which he had declared would be the precursor to building a temple (see Deut. 12:10). But God said no to his desire, not because it was a bad desire but because the Lord had chosen David's son, Solomon, to be the temple builder (2 Sam. 7:13).

It was after this refusal and promise that David committed adultery with Bathsheba and murdered her husband, Uriah (2 Sam. 11). As a consequence of his sin, his own family fell apart, with his sons committing rape, murder, and rebellion (2 Sam. 13–18). If David had been disqualified as temple-builder in 2 Samuel 7, surely he was now doubly disqualified.

But then we read a surprising story in 2 Samuel 24. We are told that God incited David to count the number of men eligible for military service in Israel and Judah. A census might sound like a prudent thing to us today, but David's general, Joab, pleaded with him not to take such a step. This is remarkable, since Joab was not known for his tender conscience—he earlier murdered a rival general, Abner (2 Sam. 3:27), and he carried out without question David's instructions to make sure Uriah, Bathsheba's husband, did not come back alive from the battle (2 Sam. 11:14–25). Yet even Joab knew that to number the troops would be an unthinkable act of rebellion against God. Israel's kings were to trust in God for their deliverance from their enemies, not to trust in the number of their chariots and fighting men (see Ps. 20:7).

Strikingly, whereas in 2 Samuel we are told that God incited David to number the troops, in the parallel passage in 1 Chronicles 21 the blame for inciting David is laid at the door of Satan. Which is it? Actually, there is no contradiction here, any more than there is in the book of Job. God is ultimately sovereign over all things, and so he is the one who allowed Satan to approach and tempt David to sin. David couldn't even refuse to trust in the Lord without the Lord's express permission!

The consequences of David's sin were disastrous for Israel. The king who should have protected his people from their enemies became the cause of their death and destruction. God offered David a choice of punishments for his sin: three years of famine on the land, three months of fleeing before his enemies, or three days of pestilence on the land (2 Sam. 24:13). In response, David asked God to delete the middle option from the list—the one that would have affected him most directly—and to choose from the remaining two. So God sent a pestilence on his own people, and David had to watch as seventy thousand people died for his transgression. We are told that David was in great distress (2 Sam. 24:14). I'm sure that was an understatement!

Then something truly surprising happened. The angel of the Lord was striking down the people by the threshing floor of Araunah the Jebusite, which was at that time just outside the walls of Jerusalem. As he saw the angel at work, David cried out to the Lord and said, "Behold, I have sinned, and I have done wickedly. But these sheep, what have they done? Please let your hand be against me and against my father's house" (2 Sam. 24:17). God answered David's prayer, and the slaughter stopped at once. Then the Lord told David to buy the threshing floor of Araunah and raise an altar there.

David's confession is precious and poignant, particularly in view of his sordid past. When he sinned with Bathsheba, David remained cold and unrepentant until after Nathan the prophet came to him to explain what he had done. This time, David's heart convicted him before he met up with the prophet (v. 10). David has grown a bit, and that is encouraging for us to see. But the real glory comes at the end of the passage. The threshing floor of Araunah that David bought in order to build an altar and offer sacrifices to atone for his own sin would later become the site where Solomon would build his temple. The man who was forbidden to build a temple to the Lord because he had shed blood was led by God *through his own experience of sin* to purchase the very piece of land upon which the temple would be built! Not only was he given the amazing privilege of buying the land and the oxen, but he personally officiated at the first sacrifices offered on this spot! Even though his sin caused the disaster, he was given the amazing privilege of mediating between God and his people.

I don't know if David knew the ramifications of that day's events, but surely it was an incredible act of God's kindness and mercy to him in spite of his sin. We don't find out whether David's heart was shattered by the outrageous nature of God's love and generosity to him, but our hearts should be. This is unbearable kindness and unbelievable love.

PETER'S STORY

The apostle Peter experienced many humiliating moments when his enthusiasm and overconfidence led him into sin. On the Mount of Transfiguration, as he foolishly suggested building three temporary shelters on the mountaintop for Jesus, Elijah, and Moses, his childish babbling was silenced by a strong word from heaven: "This is my beloved Son . . . listen to him" (Matt. 17:5). It is as if God were saying, "Stop talking, Peter! This isn't about you; it's about Jesus!" Then there was the time when he suggested to Jesus that going to the cross wasn't a particularly good idea. Jesus called him "Satan" and told him to get behind him, to stop trying to sabotage the work he came to do (Matt. 16:23). Peter received some pretty embarrassing public rebukes in his time, and he deserved them!

Nothing could compare, however, to the time in the courtyard of the high priest when, pressed by the serving girl, Peter denied even knowing Jesus (Matt. 26:69–74). Then the rooster crowed and Peter burst into tears, certain that in his fear he had committed an unpardonable sin in denying Jesus (Matt. 26:75). How do you think Peter felt when he finally encountered the risen Christ face to face once again? Surely the shame I felt over committing sexual sin is almost nothing compared to what Peter must have felt at that moment. In Jesus' hour of greatest need, Peter had rejected and abandoned him to his horrifying death.

Perhaps you too know that powerful and dreadful feeling of filth and shame when your sin has been uncovered in all its ugliness and there is nothing to say and nowhere to run. Yet now this glorious Jesus whom Peter had betrayed was risen from the dead and standing in front of him. How terrifying that must have been! Peter must have expected anger, rebuke, and even punishment. Instead Jesus did something so unexpectedly kind and generous that it was almost unbearable. Taking him aside, Jesus said to him, "Peter, feed my sheep." Three times Jesus asked Peter if he loved him and repeated to him the same commission, as it were symbolically enabling him to undo his three denials of Jesus (John 21:15–17). How kind and gracious! Peter was not only forgiven and welcomed back into the community of the disciples, but also welcomed into the heart of the one he had betrayed. He was even re-commissioned by this one who knew him inside and out to be one of the foundational apostles on whom the church would be built.

Peter was certainly not worthy of such an honor. He was a coward, a liar, and a deserter! Even after Jesus restored him, Peter would later struggle again with his fear of people in Galatia in a way that seemed to jeopardize the gospel (Gal. 2:11–14). Yet Jesus not only withheld the punishment Peter deserved, but he forgave him freely and lavished him with rich blessings and a glorious task. If that doesn't make your heart shake with awe and wonder, what will?

THE EXPULSIVE POWER OF A NEW AFFECTION

An eighteenth-century preacher named Thomas Chalmers once wrote a sermon entitled, "The Expulsive Power of a New Affection."[4] In it he argued that God is the agent of change in our lives, and unless he acts in our hearts we won't want to obey him, and even when we do we won't be able to. God uses many different means or ways of working change in us. After all, the whole universe is at his disposal, and the great Creator can be creative in the ways he goes about convicting us of sin and making us want to obey him.

I was once deeply convicted by the words of an Orthodox Jewish radio talk show host who persuaded me, by her words to a caller, that I was a selfish daughter-in-law. God used her to motivate me to ask my mother-in-law's forgiveness for my bad behavior. I didn't know it at the time, but that would be the last time I saw my mother-in-law because she died just a few years later.

Chalmers wrote of one profound way that God works to transform us into better worshipers. He goes right to the heart of the matter by discussing the role of heart idolatry in shaping the behaviors that flow from us. He notices that a young man is usually captivated by the idolatry of comfort and pleasure, and therefore he spends his nights out on the town and lies in bed until late in the afternoon. He is lost in the worship of pleasure, and he sees no need to rise early and work hard as long as he can please himself. As he grows, however, other loves may captivate his heart. He may fall in love with a woman, and new and brighter idolatries may find a home in his heart. To win her, his latest prize, his behavior will change dramatically. He will dress better and groom himself to appear attractive to her. He will become more gentle and polite, more sociable, well-kempt, and attentive.

If power or money is his idol, then perhaps it is a new job that will get him into bed early and out of bed in the morning.

He sees this job as the means to fulfill his cravings, and suddenly in order to keep this job and succeed at it he is transformed and able to do what he seemed completely unable to do just last week. Thus the affections of the heart govern behavior.

Jesus said the same thing when he taught us that all our behavior flows from the heart (Matt. 12:34–35), so that all our attempts to reform must go through the pathway of the heart. The heart is the center of worship and the home of desire, and only God can change our hearts. Have you ever tried to change your own heart? Have you tried to make yourself less angry, less bitter, more patient, or more kind? It doesn't work very well. We can change our outward behavior for short periods of time, but only God can change our hearts.

It was the same way for Old Testament Israel. Their long history of sin clearly demonstrated their total inability to change themselves and keep God's law. What they needed to please God was nothing less than a new heart. And this is exactly what God promised to give them.

> I will sprinkle clean water on you, and you shall be clean from all your uncleannesses, and from all your idols I will cleanse you. And I will give you a new heart, and a new spirit I will put within you. And I will remove the heart of stone from your flesh and give you a heart of flesh. And I will put my Spirit within you, and cause you to walk in my statutes and be careful to obey my rules (Ezek. 36:25–27).

Chalmers demonstrates that the way God changes our affections and our worship is by making Christ more and more beautiful to our souls. He melts our hearts with his endless patience, love, and forgiveness until we become people who begin to forgive others readily. The Holy Spirit shows us Christ in all his glory, and in time we become more captivated with him than we are with our silly, powerless idols. The more we see of him, the more we are changed into his image until that wonderful day when we will be like him, for we will see him face to face (1 Cor. 13:12).

GOD'S TRANSFORMING KINDNESS

The apostle Paul also knew all about this kind of unbearable love. He wasn't just an average Pharisee in his youth. On the contrary, his life's goal was to purge the world of Christians! He was present at the death of Stephen and was determined to persecute the followers of Jesus Christ (Acts 7:58–8:1). What must have been going through his mind on the day he was knocked to the ground by a bright light and came face to face with the one who he hated most? Jesus' words, "Saul, Saul, why are you persecuting me?" could not have seemed like joyful words of welcome as blindness descended upon him and his life changed forever (Acts 9:5–8). Blindness must have seemed a fitting punishment for all his attempts to extinguish the light of the world.

Yet once again, in this grand and astounding reversal, not only was Paul called and forgiven of his atrocious crimes, but he was granted the privilege of seeing Christ face to face and being made an apostle of the faith he had once so vigorously persecuted. His writings dominate the New Testament and his joy in the gospel is undeniable. He could not stop thinking about the contrast between what he deserved as a hater of the church and what he was actually given in Christ—about how the grace of God had overflowed to him with the faith and love that are in Christ Jesus even though he had once been a blasphemer, persecutor, and opponent of the faith (1 Tim. 1:12–14). No wonder he was a powerhouse of enthusiasm and strength in the face of all kinds of trials and hardships (2 Cor. 4:16–18). Thankfulness is the most powerful motivation for worship that exists.

The kindness of God is life-transforming. It was always meant to be. Have you ever been transformed by such a moment? You don't have to have committed gross outward sin to know exactly what this feels like. Newton notes that God makes some of his children examples and warnings to others by letting them fall into huge public sin.[5] For others, their worst sins will be known only to God and themselves, and yet their own hearts will nonetheless witness the tragic depths of their own depravity. Sometimes the Holy Spirit will fill you with such a sense of deep conviction over inward sin, even "small" sin, that you begin to realize what a horrible offense it is against a holy and loving God. It all becomes very personal and you see clearly how you have hated and despised the One who created and redeemed you, and you are undone by two things, "the wonder of redeeming love, and your unworthiness."[6]

Several months ago I received an interesting phone call from my newest son, Wayne. We met him while he was a student at the college where my husband teaches, and during the past six years he has become our dearly beloved, almost adopted son. He is a remarkably gifted young man who quickly developed a love for Newton's writings that is almost as deep as my own. In fact, he is the person God used to convince me to write this book. He was calling to tell me that he had just received a promotion at work. This was fabulous news, and I celebrated with him. But what captivated me even more was what he said next. He is a young man who earnestly wants to grow and change and at times feels discouraged by his sin. He said he had a terrible week in the sanctification department. In spite of his sincere desires to stop sinning, he had sinned a lot and was feeling the weight of this. Then he got the raise. He marveled that God planned this gift for him after a bad week of failure, and not after a good week of obedience. He concluded that God was kind to do this because he is prone to thinking that he must earn God's favor by obedience and that God is angry with him when he sins. This way, he could not be confused or feel entitled to it. For his own good pleasure and the delight of his redeemed son, God had freely bestowed this gift when Wayne was feeling weak and sinful. How kind of our heavenly Father to so carefully match his providences to our needs!

THE ATTITUDE OF GRATITUDE

I suppose if there were one word to describe this powerful transformation, it would be *gratitude*. Gratitude is a strong and mighty emotion that calms the spirit and restores order to the universe. To be grateful, of course, you must first be needy or want something very much. If you think you deserve whatever it is that you want, you won't be grateful when you get it; rather, you will feel that you have been reimbursed or remunerated for your effort. We rarely feel grateful when our employer deposits the agreed amount of our paycheck into our bank account. We feel entitled to it. If you really want something that you cannot afford and someone gives it to you, your gratitude is real. But what if the thing you want and crave is the direct opposite of what you deserve, and you are utterly helpless to obtain it? What if, in fact, the harder you try to get it, the further it drifts from you? How does it feel to deserve bitterness, contempt, and hatred and receive overwhelming love and acceptance instead?

In Luke chapter 7 we read of a woman who was truly grateful. In fact, she was so grateful to Jesus and so lost in love and worship before him that she behaved in a strange, even embarrassing way. She was a prostitute after all, and here she was anointing the feet of Jesus with costly perfume while weeping profusely and drying his feet with her hair (v. 38). No respectable woman would ever have acted like this in such a public setting.

When the smug, self-righteous Pharisees judged both her and Jesus for this outrage, Jesus responded by telling a story about forgiveness. Thinking about our debt in financial terms seems to make everything clearer. It was obvious to everyone that when it came to loans being forgiven, the more money you owed, the more grateful you would inevitably be when the loan was forgiven in full. Jesus said this woman loved him a great deal because she had been forgiven a great deal (Luke 7:41–48). As Newton wrote to a Miss Medhurst,

> If obedience be the thing in question, looking unto Jesus is the object that melts the soul into love and gratitude! Those who greatly love, and are greatly obliged find obedience to be easy. When Jesus is upon our thoughts, either in His humbled or His exalted state; either as bleeding on the cross or as worshiped by all the host of heaven then we can ask the apostle's question with a befitting disdain, "Shall we continue in sin that grace may abound? God forbid!" What! shall I sin against my Lord, my Love, my Friend—who once died for my sins, and now lives and reigns on my behalf! What! shall I sin against my Redeemer who supports, and leads, and guides, and feeds me every day? God forbid![7]

There is our conclusion simply stated: we are never to sin so that grace will abound, and yet, whenever we do sin, grace does abound. It is breathtaking and startling to think that the God against whom we sin so easily and frequently uses that same sin to bless us and to reveal his loving and forgiving heart toward disgusting sinners. That's what is so amazing about grace!

FOR FURTHER REFLECTION

1. In what ways have you reaped what you have sown in this life? How have you reaped what you have not sown, both negatively and positively?

2. What are the grand reversals of your story? Describe those times when you sinned and you knew you deserved exposure and punishment, but God lavished you with love and blessing instead. How did it feel?

3. In what ways have you tried to change your outward behaviors? In what ways have you tried to change your own heart? How successful have you been?

4. How have you experienced God's transforming power from the inside out? What feelings and thoughts drove your desires to change and grow?

5. Do you often feel overwhelming gratitude to God? Why or why not?

6. What are some of the stories of your life that have resulted in feelings of profound gratitude? How does gratitude tend to compel you to act?

7. Do you tend to feel guilty over your lack of gratitude to God? What is the remedy for that?

CHAPTER TWELVE

the joyful implications
of amazing grace

*Though sin wars, it shall not reign; and though it breaks
our peace, it cannot separate us from his love.*
—John Newton[1]

Recently a friend of mine walked into her first session with a biblical counselor. She sat down with a sigh and began to explain to her counselor what her week had been like. She had been wrestling with significant guilt over her sinful desires and over her weakness and inability to change, or even to want to change. However, just a few days before, God had blessed her with a rich and profound sense of her need to rest in the finished work of Christ and to give up her frantic attempts to try hard enough to do better.

The counselor smiled at her and said, "Oh, I'm not going to let you off that easily." Really? I would have given the girl a standing ovation and thrown a party to celebrate God's kindness to her and the strong work of the Holy Spirit in her heart! I would have persuaded her that the angels were dancing in heaven and wishing they could understand the marvelous and outrageous grace of God to a sinner like her. Why do we do this to each other? Why are we so afraid of grace?

There are powerful implications of the message of the gospel that we rarely talk about or hear proclaimed. They are beyond imagining as a source of comfort, peace, and joy, but we hesitate to mention them, let alone delight and frolic in them. We are terrified that too much grace equals freedom from human effort and that such a freedom will inevitably lead to debauchery, licentious living, and a loss of interest in pursuing holiness. Those are important things to think about, but they shouldn't keep us from immersing ourselves in the gifts that have been given to us in Christ. Fear is not a good foundation for godly counsel. Indeed, our fear may actually keep us from the one truth that is the most powerful motivator for change that God has given. What if being reminded that you don't have to change to win God's favor unleashes such joy and sense of safety in your soul that changing becomes the thing you desire most, simply out of gratitude for such overwhelming acceptance and love? If this is true, then holding people back from moving toward such relief and joy may be a huge stumbling block on their path to holiness.

YOUR SINS ARE FINITE IN NUMBER AND COMPLETELY PAID FOR

In the religious circle I call home we love to talk about "the doctrines of grace." We particularly love Jesus' last words from the cross, "It is finished" (John 19:30). Those three words from the lips of our dying Savior guarantee us that his work of redemption was completed on the cross. All the sins of his people, from creation into eternity, were paid for in full in that one, grand, sweeping moment of sacrificial atonement. That doctrine is so much more than a lofty theological concept to be admired or argued about. It is a riveting and life-changing truth that maps directly onto every moment of our lives. In particular, it should greatly inform every discussion we have about change. There are startling truths to be enjoyed here—truths in which Christians rarely delight, even in my favorite theological circles.

The first is the fact that, if you are united with Christ today, the number of sins you will commit in your lifetime is a finite number, and they were all paid for in full before you emerged howling from your mother's womb. Many of us have been moved by the words of the well-known hymn "It is Well with My Soul." The third verse says the following:

My sin, oh the bliss of this glorious thought
My sin, not in part but the whole
Is nailed to the cross and I bear it no more
Praise the Lord, praise the Lord, O my soul.[2]

Stop for a moment and wrap that thought around you. Do you know the utter bliss of that truth? Does it regularly settle on your heart, bringing sweet peace and joy, especially when you are continuing to struggle with sin? Your soul was purchased before you were ever conceived. Your sins may feel innumerable and overwhelming to you, but they were all known to God individually before you existed. Each one was specifically paid for before you ever thought or willed to commit it. The sins you have not yet committed are already wiped out, atoned for, and paid in full. Jesus paid it all!

This is outrageously good news, especially when the Holy Spirit begins to show you just how much you sin even in your best moments. That is because even when we are believers the natural drift of our hearts is away from God, and sin remains the constant context for our growth in obedience. In the words of Robert Robinson, we are all "prone to wander, Lord I feel it, prone to leave the God I love."[3]

Nonetheless, we do not have to agonize over each and every sin as if every individual transgression drives yet another nail into our Savior's hands. It is finished! His work was completed when he gave up his spirit, and it was accepted by the Father as our death. Every sin for each of God's people was specifically atoned for in that moment, and when the Father raised the Son to life again, that was irrefutable evidence that the payment was accepted in full.

This reality frees you from the morbid need to wallow in grief and sorrow over your sin. Jesus isn't suffering day after day for your sin. He sits triumphantly at the right hand of God and has won the final and decisive victory for you. If constant lamenting over your sin could actually help you atone for it, then it would be a noble act. However, since there is nothing to be added to your salvation and your agony contributes nothing to your salvation or sanctification, then you are free to walk through life with confidence in your forgiveness. Godly sorrow for sin does not lead to self-condemnation and attempts to atone for your sins through acts of penance. Godly sorrow leads to repentance, which leads us to the cross. There we see, once again, the beautiful sufficiency of our marvelous Savior. Godly sorrow leads us on to a big party, another glorious celebration of the truth of the gospel.

I realized the constant reality of my own sin in a fresh way while I waited to hear whether or not P&R would offer me a contract for this book. As I considered how to pray and what it would be right to ask God in this situation, I was faced with a dilemma. Trying to be godly, I thought perhaps I should begin by asking God for the outcome that would lead to the least sin on my part. I knew that a rejection would make me feel angry, resentful, fearful, and depressed, and since a contract was what I really wanted, I prayed many times that P&R would think favorably of my proposal and the committee would vote for publication.

This thought led to another one, though. How would I feel if the answer was yes? Well, elated and excited, of course! However, just because these are positive feelings doesn't mean they are sinless. I knew I would feel elation because I crave glory and notoriety and I really want to be someone. I began to realize that a positive answer to my prayer would inevitably lead me down a pathway of sin just as surely as a negative vote would. I am a sinner, and I was going to sin either way. There would be sins of anger and despair if I was disappointed, and sins of pride, drivenness, fear, and defensiveness if I got what I wanted. This is what it means to be knitted to sinful flesh while I live in this body: I will sin no matter what pathway God leads me down.

This could easily be a paralyzing dilemma, and at times I have indeed been paralyzed by just such an awareness of the presence of sin in all my thoughts and motives. Perhaps, I thought, I should withdraw the proposal completely. But wouldn't that just be seeking an easy escape? There would also be a million temptations to self-pity and self-hatred along that pathway as well. If I take my sin too hard, I may remain frozen in a wasteland that is completely focused on myself in a fearful and self-absorbed frenzy of misguided good intent. I am not supposed to want to sin or plan to sin. However, as a sinner living in a fallen world, it is inevitable that I am going to sin time and time again.

However, there are alternatives to paralysis, and clearer thinking could lead me down a different path altogether. If all my sins are already known to God and paid for by Christ, I am free to move forward trusting that God has planned which sins I will wrestle with. He already knows how he will walk through them with me and how he will use them to teach and strengthen me. I am freed from a relentless counting of wrongs to move into whatever God has decided is next for me, confident that his grace is always greater than all my sin. There is a freedom to live life joyfully, confident that I am a sinner who will sin so many times each day that I can't keep track, but that my heavenly Father is sovereign over each of those sins and that I have been set free from the vast and enormous punishment that each tiny one rightly deserves. Such freedom and pleasure in God is almost too astounding to describe or explain. It makes me want to fall to the ground in worship and wonder that I could be so well loved and cared for by my Creator!

There is a sweet sense in which the gospel helps us not to take ourselves too seriously. Though sin is ugly and our foolishness is profound, we are also free to marvel at our silliness and chuckle at how ridiculous we often are. John Newton was a man full of humor and wit who never left a room without leaving behind the rich fragrance of the gospel in some poignant way. You can catch a glimpse of this side of him in a letter he wrote to Thomas Scott, the minister who took over his church when he moved from Olney to London.

> Methinks I see you sitting in my old corner in the study. I will warn you of one thing. That room—(do not start)—used to be haunted. I cannot say I ever saw or heard anything with my bodily organs, but I have been sure there were evil spirits in it and very near me—a spirit of folly, a spirit of indolence, a spirit of unbelief, and many others—indeed their name is legion. But why should I say they are in your study when they followed me to London, and still pester me here?[4]

WE ARE DECLARED NOT GUILTY

The doctrine of our union with Christ is another truth with life-altering implications. Single imputation is fabulous; that our sins would be imputed to Christ and definitively dealt with on the cross is unimaginably wonderful. But it's not enough. Single imputation is only half the gospel, offering great comfort for the sins you have already committed but leaving you feeling discouraged and hopeless by the fact that you keep sinning. It almost makes the whole thing worse. Knowing that Jesus left heaven to live on earth and suffer such brutality in your place is a heavy emotional load to bear in the face of such ongoing weakness and inability. True believers must wrestle with the tragic sadness that "It was *my* sin that held him there,"[5] and such sorrowful emotions often lead to extreme promises of life change and obedience.

However, sad and guilty hearts don't usually find obedience any more attainable; if anything, they find it more evasive. We are people who want to feel good, and desperate feelings of real inadequacy rarely drive us to worship. Instead, they drive us to our favorite idolatries and addictions to find a thimbleful of comfort before beginning the guilty process all over again. This is not the overflowing joy of the gospel of Jesus Christ.

The exhilarating truth of our spiritual vindication jumps off the pages of Scripture with clarity all the way back in the book of Zechariah. With the benefit of New Testament hindsight, we can get a sparkling glimpse of where the story is headed, even in the shadows of the old covenant. In Zechariah 3, we encounter a courtroom scene in which the judge is the Angel of the Lord and the prosecutor is Satan himself. The defendant is Joshua, the high priest, mediator between God and his people, who have just returned from exile in Babylon. The charge against Joshua is that the man who should be righteous and clean is covered with filthy excrement.[6] God's people are in serious trouble. If the high priest is such a disastrous and guilty mess, how will he ever be able to plead for mercy on behalf of his extremely guilty people? Joshua's guilt is so self-evident that we can actually smell it on him. Satan doesn't have to say a thing!

The verdict is equally obvious: the high priest is clearly guilty as charged. Joshua needs help, and he needs it fast! Yet into that tense and dramatic silence, life-giving words of grace and mercy are spoken: "Is not this a brand plucked from the fire? . . . Remove the filthy garments from him. . . . Behold, I have taken your iniquity away from you, and I will clothe you with pure vestments" (Zech. 3:2–4).

Did you catch that? Without Satan being permitted to utter a single word, the Angel of the Lord spoke on Joshua's behalf. Satan had a legitimate case against this one, but he didn't even get a moment to describe the charge against Joshua before he was completely silenced and Joshua rescued. Joshua wasn't just acquitted on the basis of unclear evidence or an incompetent prosecution. No, he had been chosen for salvation and rescued from the fire, so he would never have to face the deadly consequences of his sin. His filthy, fecal-smeared garments were removed, signifying the removal of all his sin and guilt. But the astonishing story continued! Joshua was dressed in clean clothing that he neither owned nor deserved.

Just as his filthy clothing represented his sin, so the clean clothing that he received represents Christ's righteousness given to us by faith. Not only was Joshua's sin and guilt removed, but he was then dressed in the perfect and spotless garments of a goodness won for him by another. With that move, the story goes from being wonderful to being spectacularly joyful. Tullian Tchividjian calls this "the hilarity of unconditional grace."[7] It is unimaginable and beyond reason that God could love filthy sinners so much.

We are all just like Joshua, obviously guilty and reeking of foulness so deep and pervasive that it constantly threatens to overwhelm and bury us alive. We don't just sin a little from day to day; we sin constantly in our thoughts, in the things we actively do, and in the countless things that we should do but don't. We owe God perfect love, obedience, and worship every minute of every day, yet even the most mature Christian will fail to come close to this kind of goodness for one minute of *any* day. Our problem is extensive and hopeless, for we don't just need a moderately clean record; we need a history of perfect goodness in order to meet the demands of God's laws. Zechariah 3 shows us a visual picture of the spiritual truth that we possess in Christ. He paid the penalty for all our sin by dying on the cross, and now he wraps us moment by moment in the embrace of all his righteousness given to us. He is everything that we need, not just for salvation but for every day of our lives.

So what does that mean for you and me from day to day? It means that although we sin with every breath we take, at the same time in Christ we actually possess all the perfection we need to please God. Jesus succeeded in every way that we have failed, and though we fall wretchedly short of the obedience we need and desire, he has obeyed in our place and given us his goodness to replace our badness. At the end of a day when I can look back and see the many specific times that I have sinned in weakness or in willful rebellion, I can also see Jesus obeying for me and giving me his perfect record in each of those specific areas. There is no other way to survive my failure. I have been rescued, my sins have been dealt with decisively on the cross, and now God sees me as he sees his own Son, as a perfect lawkeeper. Isn't that delicious and extravagant grace?

Enjoy this doctrinal truth. Immerse yourself in it; delight and frolic in it. It is too wonderful to be believed, and yet it is absolutely true. But I will warn you that you are unlikely to think of it nearly as often when you are standing strong and tall in the faith. You won't think that you need it during those times. When you are severely discouraged by your sin and lack of growth, think back over the events of that day and remember the sins you have committed. Confess them to God and ask him to give you the sweet gift of repentance and faith. Then celebrate. Though each of these sins is worthy of death, you are still alive! God has not destroyed you; instead, he crushed his Son in your place. You are still here, still welcomed and cherished by your

Father in spite of all your sin. You are safe, and he is preparing a place for you with him for eternity.

Sometimes when you look at the narrative of Jesus' life, you can actually see or hear him obeying in your place. For instance, I have eating problems. I use food to sedate myself sinfully and anesthetize my painful and angry feelings. Although I have grown substantially in this area, I am still a glutton and still prone to medicating myself with food. Today I ate many things sinfully—two bowls of cereal when one would have done; an entire, huge Cadbury chocolate bar; a lunch I didn't need; and the list goes on. I am ashamed of myself, and as a result I feel awful and inclined to be mean to people around me and to eat even more! But the truth of Christ's goodness given to me has real power to rescue me in the midst of my shameful feelings of failure. Christ was a perfect eater, and his record of perfect eating is mine. He never used food sinfully, even when Satan tempted him to turn stones into bread (Matt. 4:3–4). He feasted at weddings and fasted prayerfully, thanking his Father for the good food given to him. And now, today, his obedience has replaced my sinfulness and I stand before God clean and pure. Like no other, this doctrine has the power to turn shame into worship and failure into adoration. There is nothing quite like it.

THE GENEROUS PATIENCE OF GOD

We all love the story of the prodigal son, or more precisely as it is in the Bible, the parable of the two sons (Luke 15:11–32). We are amazed and struck with wonder at the loving father who waits for his son's return and runs to greet him, forgiveness oozing from every pore when he has every right to be angry. We are even more amazed when we realize that this is a story about God and us. We are the sons, sometimes arrogant with pride and self-righteous obedience, sometimes shattered by the extent of our own sin and rebellion (see Isa.

1:2–9). Yes, our heavenly Father welcomes prodigals home time and time again.

Yet there is one remarkable aspect of the story I have never heard anyone comment on. How was the son able to run off and be so bad? It was the father who gave him the money in the first place! This is a startling truth for so many reasons! Given the nature of the culture in which the story takes place, the father's response to the son's audacious and arrogant demand to sell the family inheritance is utterly unexpected. However, I am riveted by the fact that the father gave his son the property, knowing full well what he would use the proceeds of its sale for—*sin*!

There are many sins that the son would not have been able to commit if he had lacked the funding. He would hardly have been able to travel to the far country, let alone engage in alcohol abuse, gluttony, and the use of prostitutes. Yet in the story, the father in some sense enables the son to pursue his sins.

We need to be careful in applying this insight to our relationship with God, yet the parallels are undeniable. We know that God is holy and despises all such sin, and yet, like the father in the story, he provides us with the means that we, his sons and daughters, will use to sin with abandon! Surely, if God the Father were determined to keep the total number of our sins as low as possible, one way to do it would be to restrict the means for our sin. And yet that is not what the good father does, in the story or in our lives. God never tempts anyone to sin, but he does turn us over to our sin time and time again. In fact, since we depend on him for everything, even the breath we take, we could say that he provides the means by which we will fall. What we see graphically portrayed in this parable, and in our own lives, is God using what he hates to accomplish what he loves.

Think about the good fruit that resulted from the father giving the son the resources necessary for him to live out his sinful ambitions. Had the younger son been forced to stay at home through lack of resources his outward behavior might have been restrained, but his heart would not have been changed. He would have become angrier and bitter, convinced that his father stood between him and enjoying life. By setting him free to pursue his sinful desires, the father paradoxically started him on the path that would set him free from sin's power as he saw its emptiness and bitter fruit. In this way, the younger son would learn that he who is forgiven much will surely love much. The magnitude of his sin ultimately served to soften his hard heart and heighten the glorious character of his patient and loving father.

Meanwhile, the elder brother, whose high moral standards held him back from his brother's wild adventures, never learned that truth. His obedience flowed out of exactly the same hard and bitter heart that his brother had displayed, convincing him that his father was the chief obstacle to his happiness (see v. 29). Yet his self-righteousness blinded him to his own hard and arrogant heart. There is a sobering warning to the most earnest Christians here: you may actually sin more profoundly in all of your obedience than others do in their rebellion, and you may be the one who misses the party of grace because you don't want to go in if those "sinners" are there.

Perhaps there is a lesson here for Christian parents struggling with rebellious kids, too. Sometimes in our desire to protect our kids from sin, we prevent them from understanding the depravity of their hearts. We may teach them about it and quote relevant Bible verses, but theory is different from experience. They may need to see the deep depravity that lurks within their own souls if they are ever to cherish deeply their salvation.

Like the father of the two sons in the parable, we may need to let them go and turn them over to their sin for a season so they will also discover their great need for a Savior. This seems like a terrifying thought to us since we know they can damage themselves, others, and our reputations in severe ways. Our fears are not unfounded. Sin leads to death, and our kids may inflict serious and critical harm on themselves and others around them. They may conceive children who will bear the marks of their sin for a lifetime. But just as surely as God was sovereign over the sins of the two brothers, we can trust that his protection surrounds our children. He will set limits to their disobedience and boundaries to the harm that they may do and will walk with them to protect them along the way. They cannot sin outside of his will, and he will surely walk them, and us, through the valleys of death that he calls us to walk through, guiding and comforting us all along the way. He has promised to use all things for their good, for our good, and for his glory, and we can cling to that promise even when their lives seem out of control.

GOD'S ABIDING PLEASURE

Many of the people who I counsel desperately want to know how God feels about them when they sin. They generally assume that he is pleased with them when they obey, and they wish they could live their lives more after the pattern of the elder brother. Yet since even outward obedience often seems beyond them, they are convinced that they must spend much of the time beneath God's righteous frown. If you are very aware of your sin, and you think God is angry with you every time you sin, then life becomes truly miserable. I commiserate with their pain. Since I also seem to sin constantly with my heart flaring often throughout each day, if their thinking is correct I would be condemned to a lifetime of depression. This perspective is clearly expressed in the hymn "Trust and Obey."[8]

> When we walk with the Lord in the light of his Word,
> What a glory he sheds on our way!
> While we do his good will, he abides with us still,
> And with all who will trust and obey.

Trust and obey, for there's no other way
To be happy in Jesus, but to trust and obey.

But we never can prove the delights of his love
Until all on the altar we lay;
For the favor he shows, for the joy he bestows,
Are for them who will trust and obey.

Songs like this echo certain ideas deep within our law-tortured souls. This was probably meant to be a lovely hymn about the joys of obedience to God—and obedience is indeed a joy-filled thing when it flows from a heart of gratitude. Yet is it really true that Jesus sheds his glory on our way *only* when we walk with him? Does God abide with us *only* if we do his good will? We are certainly called to walk with Christ (Col. 2:6) and abide in him (John 15:4), but the good news of the gospel lies in the fact that even when we are faithless, he is faithful (2 Tim. 2:13).

Because of that faithfulness to the faithless, the Lord sheds his glory on our way even when we are running from him. As the prophet Jonah discovered it is a glorious thing to be pursued relentlessly by the loving God of heaven and earth. He abides with us still and will never forsake us, whether we are doing his good will or not, as the psalmist discovered (Ps. 139:8–12). If there really is no other way to be happy in Jesus than to trust and obey, then I may as well give up all hope of joy now, because in spite of my best efforts there are many moments of each day when I am not trusting or obeying, even when my life looks pretty clean on the outside. Can we really never prove the delights of his love until *all* on the altar we lay? Can we not say that the delights of his love are even more evident when we sin against him but cannot separate ourselves from his love? In the entire history of mankind, who has ever gotten even close to laying all on the altar anyway? Even the greatest heroes of the Bible didn't lay everything on the altar, and I am far from being in the same category as them.

What hope is there for people like me who look at our hearts and see that we are people who often fail to trust and frequently don't even want to obey? If the favor he shows and the joy he bestows are only for those who trust and obey, while they are trusting and obeying, then my life is going to be one of abject frustration and misery as I keep trying and failing to lay it all on the altar. If that's the only way for me to be happy in Jesus, then I will have to settle for being unhappy in Jesus until I die or he comes for me.

Yet the gospel tells me about a different way to be happy in Jesus—one that rests upon what it actually means to be *in* Jesus, and which therefore brings joy and peace to deeply flawed sinners in the midst of their failure. Regardless of how we happen to be doing in the obedience department today, there is great joy and delight to be found in the fact that Jesus has trusted and obeyed in our place, and now his faith and perfect obedience are credited to us every moment of every day. To be in Christ means that whenever the Father looks at us, he sees us wrapped around with the righteousness of his Son and he is delighted.

How does God feel about his Son? I first began to understand something of God's passion for his Son when I held my own firstborn son in my arms. The feelings that filled my soul and threatened to explode all around me were not merely feelings of a mild fondness. I adored this creature with my whole body, soul, heart, and mind, and I knew that I would lay down my life for him in an instant. Jamie's birth taught me about God's love for his Son, and therefore about how God feels about me as one who is now in his Son. It wasn't the fact that Jamie was an adorable, composed, and delightful baby that won my heart. It wasn't even his big blue eyes or his engaging smile. It was the fact that he was mine. I felt this way, and continue to feel this way, about all my kids—including my oldest, almost-adopted son—because they belong to me. If I can love this way as a sinful and fallen parent, how much more love must God, the perfect parent, have for all those whom he has chosen and adopted into his family? This is a love so powerful that it defies all human logic, a love that would go to unfathomable lengths to rescue, protect, and defend the beloved. That is just what God did: he went to unimaginable lengths to have us for his own. This is unbearable, incomprehensible, life-transforming love.

God is not changeable and flaky, either. He doesn't tell us at one moment that we are safely clothed in the goodness of his Son and lavished with his love, only for his smile to be replaced with an angry frown toward us every time we fall. God cannot be angry with us. His wrath was all spent on his Son in our place, and we are told that there is now no condemnation, and therefore no anger left over for us (Rom. 8:1). God has also chosen that we should walk on this earth as weak and sinful people for now, so it would be incongruous with his nature to think that, having ordained our weakness, he will then get angry with us whenever we fall.

The Bible does use the language "grieve the Holy Spirit" to describe how God feels about us in our sin (Eph. 4:30). Once again, the parable of the prodigal son may illuminate this language. Though good human parents may feel angry when their children willfully rebel, the father in the story is not described with even a hint of anger. Rather there is sorrow and longing, combined with enormous joy when the son is spotted on the horizon (Luke 15:20–24). Not only is there no anger on the part of the father, there are also no recriminations upon the son's return. The anger and righteous indignation belong to the elder brother instead.

This is yet another way in which we are not like God. I have counseled loving Christian parents as they have walked through just such a scenario, and in their fallenness it is nearly impossible for them to bypass anger and righteous indignation at their children's behavior. I understand that, because I would be angry too. But God is not like us in this.

Likewise in Hebrews 12:5–11 we read that God disciplines the sons who he loves, and this is a precious blessing. However, our law-crushed hearts quickly read angry displeasure into discipline. In reality he has a sweet sorrow for the disciplinary pain that we will have to endure. When we let our daughter Hannah fall down the stairs, we didn't enjoy it or have revenge in mind. We were not angry or displeased with her in any way, though her persistence could be annoying! We simply acknowledged that she needed to learn something important, and that a smaller pain would be the best and quickest way for her to learn something that would protect her from greater harm. We stood back, as hard as that was for us, and then we rushed to comfort her when she fell.

Likewise, when we read that our sin can grieve the Holy Spirit, many Christians immediately assume that grief is tantamount to anger. But grief differs from anger. God is deeply compassionate toward us in our weakness, and he remembers that we are made of dust. We are the ones who keep forgetting that truth. Just as we see Jesus grieving over sin during his earthly ministry, so the Father hurts for us and with us even as he turns us over to painfully shattering life experiences. But he is not punishing us for our sin in this, nor is he angry with us. To interpret God's heart as being angry, disappointed, impatient, or exasperated with his redeemed children is to misunderstand his character profoundly. Instead, he is training us in righteousness and causing us to grow in him.

God is not in heaven wondering how we will behave and how we will respond to temptation. He is governing every circumstance for our growth and benefit. When he turns us over to our own sin in order that we might see our great need for him, he is training us in humility and dependence. This is the loving hand of our infinitely patient heavenly Father, calmly walking us through the pathways he has ordained for us. He hates sin and grieves over the pain that we inflict on ourselves, but he is not annoyed, angry, displeased, surprised, or exasperated with us. Why not? Because Jesus has obeyed perfectly for us, and now we are hidden, wrapped, and lost in the luxurious folds of his perfection.

Can the Father feel any of those negative emotions toward his Son Jesus Christ? Of course not! And since we are united to his Son, God thinks about us the same way he thinks about him—even when we sin. This astonishing love can change our lives and give us a deep and abiding joy in the midst of our continuing weakness and sin. What is more, far from leading you further into your sin, knowing this kind of love will actually make you want to obey your heavenly Father more and more.

THE ADVANTAGES OF REMAINING SIN

Magnifying the Glory of God

Newton confidently asserts that neither our secure state as believers, nor the honor and glory of God's reputation, are diminished by the sin that remains in Christians, even as they are taught to struggle against it.[9] The implications of this are thought provoking in many ways. God has not linked his own glory with our performance, but rather with the performance of his only beloved Son. The agreement made within the Trinity before time began was meant to reveal the glory of the Godhead, and man was never given the power to diminish that glory with his sin. Quite the contrary, the relentless sinfulness of man could only magnify the huge, wonderful, determined, and unshakable love that God set on his people for his own good pleasure. The glory was never meant to reside in the creature but fully in the goodness and holiness of the Creator.

Although there is a sense in which Christians who use the gospel as an excuse to enjoy sinning bring dishonor on the Lord's name here on earth (Rom. 2:23), it is not so with those who hate their sin and yet continue to struggle with it day after day. On the contrary, Newton claims that there is a unique glory in their struggle, and every attempt is precious to God regardless of the success or failure that he has assigned to it.[10] God teaches his people to mourn over their sin and to wrestle and strive against it. However, they are invited to do so with the certain knowledge that though sin wars against believers, it will never reign. Though it can shatter their peace and joy, it can never separate them from God or pluck them from his heart or hand. In only a little while, when they are freed from weakness through death, they shall be made fully perfect.

God's good reasons for making us feel our own depravity are many. By showing us our sin, God's own power, wisdom, faithfulness and love are more dramatically displayed to us and to a watching world. His power in saving and keeping his own children in the midst of so much opposition is magnified. Newton compares this to a fire burning under water or to a burning bush that is not consumed by the flame.[11] It is nothing short of miraculous that God can so easily carry on his will regardless of the odds that are stacked against the believer.

Satan is also tormented and set in his proper place by God's power to set boundaries to his rage and limits to the damage he can do. Though Satan attacks, he cannot win. When he knocks us down, we will always rise in repentance because the Lord is on our side. Satan's failure to overcome us is all the more striking given our weakness and inability to resist him. Satan is humbled and stripped of his imagined power before the hosts of heaven, while God holds onto us in spite of all Satan's success and influence. What a hilarious thing to imagine!

Increasing Believers' Love for God

Furthermore, in this way the Lord Jesus becomes more and more precious to the redeemed soul. All boasting is completely excluded and the glory of a free and full salvation is given to Jesus alone. There is no room for co-boasting, for if we are completely dependent on Christ for both the will to obey and the ability to do so, then all of our sin remains our fault while all the credit for obedience must go to him alone. Those who sin much are forgiven much, and they grow to love their Savior more than if they had never sinned or needed his goodness in their place. Believers who are convinced of their own weakness and depravity will not—dare not—take the credit for any goodness in them at all.

Instead, they readily acknowledge that if God had not held onto them, they would have run from him at every opportunity. They would have destroyed themselves many times over again if Christ had not been their shepherd. When they wandered he brought them back. When they fell over and over again he raised them up and gave them courage to try once again. When they were sick he healed them, and when they were exhausted and weary and thought that they could never go on he revived them. Their weakness has been swallowed up in his strength, and some of the clearest proofs they have had of his beauty and excellence have been triggered by the most mortifying glimpses they have had of themselves and their own depravity.

Growing Believers' Humility

God loves a humble and contrite spirit, and this can come to us in no other way than through our own repeated sinful failure. It is interesting to read Psalm 51 in light of David's sin with Bathsheba. David's humble dependence upon God is clearly expressed as he confesses his sin and asks God to give him what he cannot make for himself. He says, "Create in me a clean heart, O God, and renew a right spirit within me. . . . Restore to me the joy of your salvation, and uphold me with a willing spirit" (Ps. 51:10, 12). David now understands in a new way that he can't make his own heart obedient or willing to submit to God. These good things require the work of God himself on David's behalf. David concludes that when God does this work, David will teach transgressors God's ways so that sinners will return to the Lord (v. 13). Like Peter, David was more qualified to lead people to a loving heavenly Father after he had seen the depths of his own sin and his great need for the power of God to work in him.

A deep sense of our own sinfulness also checks our pride and defensiveness. Whoever is truly humbled will not become easily angered when criticism comes his way, whether justified or unjustified. He knows that the real truth of his depravity is far deeper than anyone can see, and he will not quibble with those who point out his wrongs or falsely accuse him. He is worse than anyone knows but God, and he thanks God if the worst of his offenses are known only to God and to himself. Repeat offenders need to repent often so they become more compassionate and tender toward the struggles of their fellow sinners and so they learn to walk alongside them with greater love and patience. We come to know that if we seem stronger or smarter than others in a particular area, it is only grace that has made the difference. We understand that where others are weak, the seeds of the same kind of sin reside deeply in our own hearts, and apart from the grace and will of God we are capable of anything and everything.

Increasing Believers' Longing for Heaven

Newton also included in his discussion on the advantages of remaining sin the observation that we human beings aren't people who tend to long for heaven naturally. We are earth-bound and tied tightly to our possessions and to the people we can see and touch. However, when we become weary of our sin and exhausted by our inability to fight against it, our thoughts turn increasingly toward the coming day of our deliverance.[12] Newton saw God's kindness to us in this. Death is scary business, even for those who are strong in faith. We live most of our lives in denial of its approach because we can't bear to be separated from what we love on earth, and we're not quite sure of what lies ahead. However, in love, God wearies us with ourselves and helps us to long for what we naturally fear and dread.

I see this happening in my own parents now. God has blessed them with many wonderful and healthy years together in his service. Now, however, many of their closest friends have died, and they seem to live their lives in a state of perpetual gratitude and expectation. They can't wait to depart and be with the Lord. My dad is so eager for this that he says his final good-byes to me each time I drive away from his home after a visit. They both talk about death with wonder and anticipation, and they are not even sick or infirm. They find their thoughts drifting to heaven and imagining what it will be like to stand before God and see the face of their precious Savior. They have become so heavenly minded that I feel a need to remind them, every now and then, that it's not quite time for the death watch yet! Death has already lost its sting and seems to hold a great deal of fascination and anticipated joy for them. This may seem like craziness, yet it is completely and beautifully sane. As Newton himself put it,

> It is a great thing to die; and, when flesh and heart fail, to have God for the strength of our heart, and our portion forever. I know whom I have believed, and he is able to keep that which I have committed against that great day. Henceforth there is laid up for me a crown of righteousness, which the Lord, the righteous Judge, shall give me that day.[13]

These are just a few of the joyful implications of the kind of love and forgiveness that has been won for us by Jesus Christ!

FOR FURTHER REFLECTION

1. Do you ever feel a frantic need to restrain sin in yourself and others? Are you afraid of too much grace? Why or why not?

2. Do you tend to wallow in shame and sorrow when you sin? Which sins do you tend to grieve over most? Why?

3. In general, do you think you are more like the elder or the younger brother in the story of the two sons? Or perhaps both? Why?

4. Looking back over your day, in what ways can you celebrate the specific imputed righteousness of Christ for you? How have you failed, and how did he succeed in your place?

5. Do you think God is angry with you when he lets you experience the earthly consequences of your sin here and now? How might this be a kind and loving thing for him to do?

6. How does your ongoing sin reveal God's glory? In what ways has it made you more humble? How has it made you more compassionate and tender?

7. Do you long for heaven? Why or why not? How does indwelling sin change your views of death and heaven?

CHAPTER THIRTEEN

from here to eternity

*When the treble is praise, and heart humiliation for the
bass, the melody is pleasant and the harmony is good.
In this way they go through life sorrowful, yet always
rejoicing.* —John Newton[1]

I f all this is true, how are we to live our lives from day to day?
What difference should knowing these truths make in your
life here and now? The answer is that it should make all the
difference in the world!

Jesus said that he came so that we might have abundant
joy (John 15:11), not just in the life to come but now. Surely this
world is still a wilderness, and perfect peace and joy must wait for
heaven, but joy is the great result of taking your eyes off yourself
and constantly looking to Christ, whether you are standing or
falling. John Newton approached all of life with such a steady
confidence in the Holy Spirit that his outlook was unshakably
joyful. This is no small thing. Sin is big and ugly, and it hurts
people badly. How on earth could he, and can we, witness its
ravaging effects with anything but fear and dread?

If we are going to trust in our own ability to cooperate with
God for the answer, we can never know God's peace. Newton
paints for us a realistic picture of the Christian life as one that will

include many slips and falls until we reach heaven, with some of these falls having devastating consequences. God turns us over to our sin, sometimes for brief periods of time, sometimes for long seasons of dryness, apathy, and outright rebellion. However, if the Holy Spirit is carefully and lovingly managing all our falls into sin and using them for God's glory and our good, then there is great cause for joy and peace whether you are leaping forward or crawling through the Christian life. I could not counsel anyone if I did not believe this with all my heart. My hope and confidence is not in someone's ability or willingness to sanctify themselves, but rather in the Holy Spirit's work within them. If this person is a believer in Christ, then I know that the Holy Spirit has begun a good work within them that he will bring to completion on the last day (Phil. 1:6). Whether they wish it or not, the Holy Spirit's work within them cannot be frustrated.

At the same time, however much progress we make in this life, we will always fall far short of God's perfect and holy standard.[2] On the last day we will all stand before God and celebrate the fact that there is no condemnation for those who are in Christ Jesus (Rom. 8:1) and that all of the goodness we need is found in Christ alone and not in ourselves.

If the Christian life is made up of times when God is at work to will and to do (Phil. 2:13), times when he is at work to will but not to do, and times when it seems that he is doing neither, what are we called to do today? Newton is firm and clear about the portion that is assigned to us. We are to strive for growth with all our strength and to work to put sin to death within us. But we are to do so in a way that is always mindful of our inability and weakness so that we do not despair.

Newton leads us to the ordinary means of grace whereby God gives himself to us in the preaching of the Word and the ministry of the Lord's Supper.[3] We are called to be faithful participants in church worship, whether or not it feels good. There will be times when God uses church services to warm your soul and melt your heart and almost slay you with an unbearable sense of his love for you. At other times, perhaps more often, the service will be somewhat engaging and interesting, and still other times it will seem downright boring. It doesn't matter, because on each of these occasions God is at work in you, sometimes showing you what he can do in you and for you, and sometimes showing you just how unable you are to worship him on your own.

Newton muses that we cannot know why God doesn't trust us with strong and warm emotions very often and in fact seems most often to give such feelings to the youngest and most immature of Christians.[4] Perhaps it is because he sees that we easily come to treasure these experiences too much and demand them. The Lord gives experiences of his closeness or withholds them as he sees fit, but he has promised to be with us by means of faithful preaching and the Lord's Supper, regardless of emotions.

This is very practical counsel. Are you a weak and weary pilgrim? Have you reached the conclusion that this life is a difficult wilderness and you need all the help you can get just to hang in there? Then go where you can hear the Scriptures proclaimed faithfully and regularly. Come to the Lord's Table as often as you can to be reminded that the battle has been won for you and that you stand approved by God in the righteousness of another. There at Christ's table you will find real food to feed your soul and strengthen you for the journey: the body of Christ that has been broken and his blood that has been shed for you. As we come to the Table, we join together with what Dietrich Bonhoeffer calls "the fellowship of the undevout." There is no other way to receive this meal than as sinners. It speaks to us, Bonhoeffer says,

> [of] the grace of the Gospel, which is so hard for the pious to understand. . . . It confronts us with the truth and says: You are a sinner, a great, desperate sinner; now come, as the sinner

that you are, to God who loves you. He wants you as you are; He does not want anything from you, a sacrifice, a work; He wants you alone. "My son, give me thine heart" (Prov. 23:26). God has come to you to save the sinner. Be glad![5]

We desperately need to surround ourselves with brothers and sisters in Christ who are truly honest about their sin. Like John Newton, they can remind us of the gospel time and time again. These are people who won't be surprised by your sin when you confess it. They will say, "Of course you sinned.... Come with me to the throne of grace to celebrate the love of your Savior and to find help in your time of need. Now let me help you understand your heart so that you may continue to try to obey God."

HOW SHOULD YOU THINK OF YOURSELF?

By God's grace we are not left alone to try to figure out how we should view ourselves as sinners who have been saved entirely by God's grace and mercy. Let us look once again at what Paul has to say in Romans 12.

I appeal to you therefore, brothers, by the mercies of God, to present your bodies as a living sacrifice, holy and acceptable to God, which is your spiritual worship. Do not be conformed to this world, but be transformed by the renewal of your mind, that by testing you may discern what is the will of God, what is good and acceptable and perfect. For by the grace given to me I say to everyone among you not to think of himself more highly than he ought to think, but to think with sober judgment, each according to the measure of faith that God has assigned. (Rom. 12: 1–3)

First, notice this: Paul begins by issuing a strong command to radical obedience. "Present your bodies as a living sacrifice." This command makes it clear that we are not at all passive in our sanctification. There are things we need to try hard to do, acts of obedience that we need to pursue. Similarly in Ephesians 4:22–24, Paul tells us to put off our old ways and put on the new, stressing clearly our activity.

At the same time, both passages make it clear just how dependent all of our activity is on God for any and every success. We can't renew our own minds (Eph. 4:23), nor do we get to decide the measure of our faith (Rom. 12:3). Paul goes on in Romans 12 to talk about the different gifts we have been given for the sake of the body (vv. 5–8), and these too are not up to us to decide; they are a grace that we have been given. Remember, it was Walt Disney, not God, who declared that you could be whatever you want to be.

The truth is that God decides how much faith each one of us will have, how much grace we will receive, and what gifts we will possess. We must therefore think of ourselves with serious and sober consideration and live according to what has been given to us, rather than envying the gifts of others and complaining about what we have not been given. This is hard but wonderful at the same time. It can be difficult to live in the body of Christ and notice that other people are stronger in faith and far more gifted than we are. Yet God has assigned the measure of faith that each one of us will receive, and he calls us to live accordingly. That means we have no reason to be proud if we have strong faith and no reason to be ashamed if we have weak faith.

LIVING IN COMMUNITY

Deciding how much faith you have isn't something you should do by yourself. You need help and objectivity because we are profoundly blind to ourselves. Live in the community of faith and let others help you see yourself clearly. This is important, because if we think we are stronger than we are, we will constantly put ourselves in impossible positions and then feel discouraged when we fall. Some people have been given strong faith and an abundance of self-control. Yet that very strength can make it hard for them to be compassionate toward those who lack these gifts. I recently learned of a well-known pastor who described sanctification as primarily a matter of deciding to get out of bed in the morning, putting your feet on the ground, and plodding off to your quiet time. Apparently God has given him the strength and grace to do this faithfully every morning, which is wonderful. Yet he thinks that God has given everyone this same ability, and if they would just obey and do it they would be as godly and sanctified as he is. I don't have that kind of grace, and for some people just the act of getting out of bed at all will be a huge victory of God's grace, let alone plodding off for a quiet time. We need help to understand our weaknesses and protect ourselves in areas where we are vulnerable. We also need help to know when we are crushing others with the abilities God has given to us and when our expectations of others are unrealistic and harmful.

As Paul makes clear, different people have different gifts and even different amounts of faith. This is not because some Christians are in line with God's will while others are behind the curve, but rather because *that is how God designed it*. It is not coincidental that Paul's discussion leads to his teaching about different gifts given to the members of the body of Christ. God has given to some Christians great strengths and great faith to fulfill the callings that he has for them in the body. I couldn't possibly do what these people do, and I don't have to. I don't need to live in shame and despair that these people are stronger than I am in so many ways. I'm pretty weak in many areas, yet I have been given the faith and the strength to do everything that God has called me to do by his grace and through the enabling and renewing power of his Spirit.

The more you come to admire God's wisdom and believe in his love and kindness to each of us, the freer you will be from envying those with more faith and stronger gifts and from feeling superior to those who are weaker than you. God knows what he is doing, and he does all things well in the body.

John Newton points out how God could have fashioned the perfect minister by combining the preaching skills of Rev. _____ with the evangelistic gift of Rev. _____, adding the people skills of Rev. _____ and the administrative prowess of Rev. _____ (you can fill in the blanks for yourself).[6] Yet he has not chosen to give his church such a perfect man of God to lead it, but rather has given a multiplicity of gifted and flawed messengers from him. As a result, we all need the body of Christ to get us through this life. You need stronger people to strengthen and help you, and you need weaker people to love and encourage along the way. You need the help of others to open your eyes when you are caught in patterns of sin. You need their help to come alongside you and to point you to Jesus Christ as your only hope in life and death. If you are weak, you need the church of Jesus Christ. If you are strong, you need the church of Jesus Christ (Rom. 15:1).

RESTING AND RUNNING

For as long as you remain in your body of flesh, living on earth, you are called to do two things, neither of which you can do in your own strength. You are called to run the race like a champion athlete (1 Cor. 9:24), and you are called to rest in Christ (Matt. 11:28–30). These are not two separate but equal callings, as if we must constantly try to strive *and* rest at the same time. On that approach, all our striving will consume our resting and we will live our lives in a swirl of ceaseless activity, perpetual service to God, and countless self-salvation strategies. Rather, resting must be primary, for according to the author of Hebrews it is the goal of our striving. He says,

So then, there remains a Sabbath rest for the people of God, for whoever has entered God's rest has also rested from his works as God did from his. Let us therefore strive to enter that rest, so that no one may fall by the same sort of disobedience. (Heb. 4:9–11)

In Matthew 11 Jesus said, "Come unto me, all you who are weary and burdened, and I will give you rest. Take my yoke upon you and learn from me, for I am gentle and humble in heart, and you will find rest for your souls. For my yoke is easy and my burden is light." Rest must be the primary paradigm, for even if we strive with all our might for obedience we will always need the righteousness of Christ to stand in our place. No goodness of our own will ever be good enough; even in our best moments our righteousness is like filthy rags (Isa. 64:6). If we are to stand before God we must be constantly hidden in the royal robes of his goodness.

We know this for sure because, although we will be busy in heaven, it is portrayed for us as the Sabbath rest that never ends. Our chief theme for all eternity will be rest and delight in our Savior, so as we seek to enjoy a foretaste of heaven on earth now our primary goal should be to understand what it means to rest and delight in the finished work of Christ. What better way to get the courage and strength to keep running the difficult race than to rest supremely in Christ even as we set about the serious work of obedience?

Ask God to show you Christ in all his glory and beauty so that your soul drinks deeply of him. Meditate on him and fill yourself with him. Fill your mind with God's Word and with the writings of godly men and women who exalt Christ and point you to him as your only hope. Reading the Bible and other great literature won't guarantee your ability to rest in Christ; you will still need a fresh act of the Holy Spirit to make you able and willing to read good books, and you will need his work to open your eyes to understand. But if you come to believe that you are completely dependent on him for all things you will find yourself praying more and more, talking to God constantly, and asking him to do for you what you cannot do for yourself.

LOOKING TO CHRIST

You also need to see the cross of Christ often in order to think of yourself properly. The cross reminds you that you are a cherished child and a treasured possession. Even while you were a lost sinner God set his love upon you and sent his Son to die for you (Rom. 5:8). For his own pleasure the Father chose you before the world was made, and for his own joy Jesus Christ considered it worth suffering brutal torture and separation from his beloved Father in order to win you for himself. The Holy Spirit is devoted to your spiritual welfare, working in you ceaselessly, conforming you gradually to the beautiful image of Christ in many ways. You are dearly loved, completely saved, and will one day possess unimaginable beauty and glory, for you will see your Savior face to face and you will be like him.

From now until then the triune God will oversee your growth every step of the way and carry it out meticulously. We don't all get to the same place in this life, or see the same truths, or arrive at the same conclusions. God has chosen for it to be that way, perhaps to remind us that we are not saved by the correctness of our opinions, however important truth is. But there is a day coming when we will all be perfect and complete and in wonderful agreement. Nothing can prevent that from happening. You cannot decide not to be sanctified, nor can Satan or your circumstances prevail against you. You are safe, and you are loved.

John Newton reached this same conclusion about himself: "But though my disease is grievous, it is not desperate; I have a gracious and infallible Physician. I shall not die, but live, and declare the works of the Lord."[7]

The gospel is not ultimately about us and what we can and can't do or what we will or won't do. It is all about Christ and what he has done to rescue lost sinners and make them fellow heirs of eternal life. May God give us hearts that join Newton increasingly in celebrating the extravagant and incomparable love of God to us in Christ!

> O the comfort! We are not under law but under grace. The gospel is a dispensation for sinners, and we have an Advocate with the Father. *There* is the unshaken ground of hope. A reconciled Father, a prevailing Advocate, a powerful Shepherd, a compassionate Friend, a Savior who is able and willing to save to the uttermost. He knows our frame; he remembers that we are dust; and has opened for us a new and blood-besprinkled way of access to the throne of grace, that we may obtain mercy, and find grace to help in every time of need.[8]

FOR FURTHER REFLECTION

1. Are you afraid of sin—your own or others'? In what ways should you fear sin and in what ways shouldn't you?

2. Have you experienced times when it seemed that God was not working in you at all? How did it feel? How did it end? What did you learn?

3. What are you experiencing right now? Are your affections strong and your desires for God high, or are you in a wilderness of apathy and lethargy? What might God be up to in all of this?

4. What are you called to do even when he doesn't seem to be giving you the will or ability to obey? In what ways has he promised to minister to your soul?

5. How does God use the preaching of his Word and the Lord's Supper to strengthen you for your wilderness journey? Do you partake of the Lord's Supper often?

6. How has the body of Christ helped you to form an accurate assessment of yourself? How have you been a blessing to the weak, and how have believers with stronger faith been a blessing to you?

7. Are you better at running the race of faith or at resting in the finished work of Christ?

8. Do you think of the cross of Christ often? In what real and tangible ways are you in need of it every day?

Notes

Chapter One: Welcome to Your Heart

1. John Newton, "Grace in the Blade," *Select Letters of John Newton* (repr., Edinburgh: Banner of Truth, 2011), 6.

2. Robert Robinson, "Come Thou Fount of Every Blessing," 1758.

Chapter Two: Babes in Christ

1. John Newton, "Grace in the Blade," *Select Letters of John Newton* (repr., Edinburgh: Banner of Truth, 2011), 4. The description of the immature believer in this chapter is largely based on this letter.

2. John Newton, *The Life and Spirituality of John Newton* (Vancouver: Regent College Publishing, 2003), 17.

3. Ibid., 50.

4. Ibid., 36.

5. Ibid., 56.

6. Newton, "Grace in the Blade," *Select Letters of John Newton*, 4.

7. Ibid., 6.

8. John Newton, "The Full Corn in the Ear," *Select Letters of John Newton* (repr., Edinburgh: Banner of Truth, 2011), 17.

9. Newton, "Grace in the Blade," *Select Letters of John Newton*, 6.

Chapter Three: Maturing in Faith

1. John Newton, "Grace in the Ear," *Select Letters of John Newton* (repr., Edinburgh: Banner of Truth, 2011), 9. The description of the growing believer in this chapter is largely based on this letter.

2. Ibid,, 9.

3. Martin Luther, "Preface to St. Paul's Epistle to the Romans," in John Dillenburger ed., *Martin Luther: Selections from His Writing* (New York: Anchor, 1962). See also Newton's comments in "The Practical Influence of Faith," *Select Letters of John Newton* (repr., Edinburgh: Banner of Truth, 2011), 91.

4. John Newton, "Advantages From Remaining Sin," *Select Letters of John Newton* (repr., Edinburgh: Banner of Truth, 2011), 153.

5. Ibid., 153.

6. Newton, "Grace in the Ear," *Select Letters of John Newton*, 9.

7. John Newton, "Difference Between Acquired and Experimental Knowledge," *Select Letters of John Newton* (repr., Edinburgh: Banner of Truth, 2011), 138.

8. Newton, "Advantages From Remaining Sin," *Select Letters of John Newton*, 153.

Chapter Four: Grown-ups in Faith

1. John Newton, "The Full Corn in the Ear," *Select Letters of John Newton* (repr., Edinburgh: Banner of Truth, 2011), 15. The description of the mature believer in this chapter is largely based on this letter.

2. Ibid., 16.

3. "Introduction," *Select Letters of John Newton* (repr., Edinburgh: Banner of Truth, 2011), xii. The reference is to "Letter 7 to Mr. B___," *The Works of John Newton*, vol. 1 (repr., Edinburgh: Banner of Truth, 1985), 631.

4. John Newton, "The Causes, Nature and Marks of a Decline in Grace," *Select Letters of John Newton* (repr., Edinburgh: Banner of Truth, 2011), 133.

5. Newton, "The Full Corn in the Ear," *Select Letters of John Newton*, 17.

6. See John Newton, "Difference Between Acquired and Experimental Knowledge," *Select Letters of John Newton* (repr., Edinburgh: Banner of Truth, 2011), 139.

Chapter Five: The Disney Delusion

1. See John Newton, "Man in His Fallen Estate (1)," *Select Letters of John Newton* (repr., Edinburgh: Banner of Truth, 2011), 117.

2. John Newton, "How Sweet the Name of Jesus Sounds," *The Works of John Newton*, vol. 3 (repr., Edinburgh: Banner of Truth, 1985), 370.

Chapter Six: Saints and Sinners

1. John Newton, "Evil Present with the Believer," *Select Letters of John Newton* (repr., Edinburgh: Banner of Truth, 2011), 147.

2. Ibid., 146.

3. Ibid., 147.

4. Newton, "The Believer's Inability on Account of Remaining Sin," *Select Letters of John Newton* (repr., Edinburgh: Banner of Truth, 2011), 142.

5. Newton, "Difference Between Acquired and Experimental Knowledge," *Select Letters of John Newton* (repr., Edinburgh: Banner of Truth, 2011), 138.

6. Newton, "Man in His Fallen Estate (1)," *Select Letters of John Newton*, (repr., Edinburgh: Banner of Truth, 2011), 120.

7. Joni Eareckson Tada and Steven Estes, *When God Weeps: Why Our Sufferings Matter to the Almighty* (Grand Rapids: Zondervan, 1997), 69.

8. Newton, "Difference Between Acquired and Experimental Knowledge," *Select Letters of John Newton*, 138.

Chapter Seven: Discovering Your Depravity

1. John Newton, "The Advantages of Remaining Sin," *Select Letters of John Newton* (repr., Edinburgh: Banner of Truth, 2011), 153.

2. Ibid.

Chapter Eight: Grace to Fall

1. Nate Larkin, *Samson and the Pirate Monks: Calling Men to Authentic Brotherhood* (Nashville: Nelson, 2006), 73.

2. John Newton, "Grace in the Ear," *Select Letters of John Newton* (repr., Edinburgh: Banner of Truth, 2011), 9.

3. John Newton, "Advantages of Remaining Sin," *Select Letters of John Newton* (repr., Edinburgh: Banner of Truth, 2011), 152.

4. In fact, the Greek here is plural: Satan has demanded to sift all of the disciples, not only Peter. Jesus prays for us too, that our faith may not fail in the midst of our greatest failures. I am indebted to Dale Ralph Davis for this insight.

Chapter Nine: Standing in Christ Alone

1. John Newton, "Causes, Nature and Marks of a Decline in Grace," *Select Letters of John Newton* (repr., Edinburgh: Banner of Truth, 2011), 134.

2. Newton, "The Believer's Inability on Account of Remaining Sin," *Select Letters of John Newton* (repr., Edinburgh: Banner of Truth, 2011), 144.

3. See his "Letter 15" from "Twenty-six letters to a Nobleman," *The Works of John Newton*, vol. 1 (repr., Edinburgh: Banner of Truth, 1985), 490.

4. *Belgic Confession*, Article 24: "The Sanctification of Sinners."

5. The full quote is as follows: "If you are a preacher of grace, then preach a true and not a fictitious grace; if grace is true, you must bear a true and not a fictitious sin. God does not save people who are only fictitious sinners. Be a sinner and sin boldly, but believe and rejoice in Christ even more boldly, for he is victorious over sin, death, and the world. As long as we are here [in this world] we have to sin. This life is not the dwelling place of righteousness, but, as Peter says, we look for new heavens and a new earth in which righteousness dwells. It is enough that by the riches of God's glory we have come to know the Lamb that takes away the sin of the world. No sin will separate us from the Lamb, even though we commit fornication and murder a thousand times a day. Do you think that the purchase price that was paid for the redemption of our sins by so great a Lamb is too small? Pray boldly—you too are a mighty sinner." See Martin Luther, "Letter to Melanchthon, 1 August 1521," in Gottfried Krodel, trans., *Luther's Works*, vol. 48 (Philadelphia: Fortress, 1963), 281–82.

6. John Newton, "Grace in the Ear," *Select Letters of John Newton* (repr., Edinburgh: Banner of Truth, 2011), 10.

7. John Newton, "The Practical Influence of Faith," *Select Letters of John Newton* (repr., Edinburgh: Banner of Truth, 2011), 91.

8. John Newton, "What the Believer Can Attain to in This Life," *Select Letters of John Newton* (repr., Edinburgh: Banner of Truth, 2011), 159.

9. John Newton, "Advantages from Remaining Sin," *Select Letters of John Newton* (repr., Edinburgh: Banner of Truth, 2011), 152.

10. See David Powlison, "Making All Things New: Restoring Pure Joy to the Sexually Broken," in John Piper & Justin Taylor, eds., *Sex and the Supremacy of Christ* (Wheaton, IL: Crossway, 2005), 81.

11. Tullian Tchividjian, *Jesus + Nothing = Everything* (Wheaton, IL: Crossway, 2011), 24.

Chapter Ten: Suffering Sinners

1. Quoted in Richard Cecil, "Memoirs of the Rev. John Newton," *The Works of John Newton*, vol. 1 (repr., Edinburgh: Banner of Truth, 1985), 105.

2. Ibid.

3. See John Piper, "Insanity and Spiritual Songs in the Soul of a Saint," January 29, 1992, http://www.desiringgod.org/resource-library /biographies/insanity-and-spiritual-songs-in-the-soul-of-a-saint.

4. John Newton, "The Full Corn in the Ear," *Select Letters of John Newton* (repr., Edinburgh: Banner of Truth, 2011), 16. See also Grant Gordon, ed., *Wise Counsel: John Newton's Letters to John Ryland Jr.* (Edinburgh: Banner of Truth, 2009), 34-35.

5. See John Newton, "Temptation," *Select Letters of John Newton* (repr., Edinburgh: Banner of Truth, 2011), 102–10.

6. John Newton, "Grace in the Ear," *Select Letters of John Newton* (repr., Edinburgh: Banner of Truth, 2011), 11.

7. John Newton, "Letter 16 to Rev. Mr. S," *The Works of John Newton*, vol. 6 (repr., Edinburgh: Banner of Truth, 1985), 195.

8. Charles Wesley, "And Can it Be?," 1738.

9. Newton, "Letter 16 to Rev. Mr. S," *The Works of John Newton*, vol. 6, 195.

Chapter Eleven: Unbearable Love

1. John Newton, "Grace in the Ear," *Select Letters of John Newton* (repr., Edinburgh: Banner of Truth, 2011), 13.

2. See the Westminster Confession of Faith, 5.5

3. See John Newton, *Life and Spirituality, The Life and Spirituality of John Newton* (Vancouver: Regent College Publishing, 2003), 38–55.

4. Thomas Chalmers, "The Expulsive Power of a New Affection," *Sermons and Discourses* (New York: Robert Carter & Brothers, 1877), 2.271–77.

5. Newton, "Grace in the Ear," *Select Letters of John Newton*, 11.

6. Elizabeth Clephane, "Beneath the Cross of Jesus," 1872.

7. Newton, "Letter 1 to Miss M*****," *The Works of John Newton*, vol. 6 (repr., Edinburgh: Banner of Truth, 1985), 6.

Chapter Twelve: The Joyful Implications of Amazing Grace

1. John Newton, "Advantages From Remaining Sin," *Select Letters of John Newton* (repr., Edinburgh: Banner of Truth, 2011), 151.

2. Horatio Spafford, "It Is Well With My Soul," 1873.

3. Robert Robinson, "Come Thou Fount of Every Blessing," 1757.

4. Quoted in Richard Cecil, *The Life of John Newton*, ed. Marylynn Rouse (Tain, UK: Christian Focus, 2000), 145.

5. Stuart Townend, "How Deep the Father's Love For Us," © 1995 Thankyou Music.

6. See Iain Duguid, "No Condemnation," in Dennis E. Johnson, ed., *Heralds of the King: Christ-Centered Sermons in the Tradition of Edmund P. Clowney* (Wheaton, IL: Crossway, 2009), 136.

7. Tullian Tchividjian, "Presumption Produces Self-Deception," *The Gospel Coalition Blog*, last modified January 21, 2013, http://thegospelcoalition.org/blogs/tullian/2013/01/21/presumption-produces-self-deception-2/.

8. John H. Sammis, "Trust and Obey," 1887.

9. Newton, "Advantages From Remaining Sin," *Select Letters of John Newton*, 150.

10. Newton, "What the Believer Can Attain to in This Life," *Select Letters of John Newton* (repr., Edinburgh: Banner of Truth, 2011), 159.

11. Newton, "Advantages From Remaining Sin," *Select Letters of John Newton*, 151.

12. Newton, "The Believer's Inability on Account of Remaining Sin," *Select Letters of John Newton* (repr., Edinburgh: Banner of Truth, 2011), 144–45.

13. Quoted in Richard Cecil, "Memoirs of the Rev. John Newton," *The Works of John Newton*, vol. 1 (repr., Edinburgh: Banner of Truth, 1985), 89.

Chapter Thirteen: From Here to Eternity

1. "Introduction," *Select Letters of John Newton* (repr., Edinburgh: Banner of Truth, 2011), xii. The reference is to "Letter 7 to Mr.

B____," in *The Works of John Newton* (repr., Edinburgh: Banner of Truth, 1985), 1.631.

2. This perspective caused a sharp breach between Newton and John Wesley, who taught a form of perfectionism. Bruce Hindmarsh comments, "The claim to perfection, however hedged about by talk of grace, seemed [to Newton] in many cases no more than an enthusiastic self-righteousness that belied trusting wholly in the merits of Christ for redemption" ("'I Am a Sort of Middle-Man': The Politically Correct Evangelicalism of John Newton," in George Rawlyk and Mark Noll, eds., *Amazing Grace: Evangelicalism in Australia, Britain, Canada, and the United States* [Grand Rapids: Baker Book House, 1993], 43).

3. John Newton, "Causes, Marks and Nature of a Decline in Grace," *Select Letters of John Newton* (repr., Edinburgh: Banner of Truth, 2011), 135.

4. Ibid.

5. Dietrich Bonhoeffer, *Life Together*, trans. John W. Doberstein (New York: Harper & Bros., 1954), 111.

6. Richard Cecil, "Memoirs of the Rev. John Newton," *The Works of John Newton*, vol. 1 (repr., Edinburgh: Banner of Truth, 1985), 107.

7. John Newton, "Evil Present with the Believer," *Select Letters of John Newton* (repr., Edinburgh: Banner of Truth, 2011), 149.

8. Newton, "What the Believer Can Attain to in This Life," *Select Letters of John Newton* (repr., Edinburgh: Banner of Truth, 2011), 159–60.

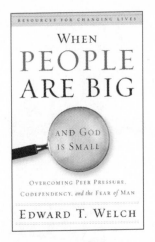

"Need people less. Love people more. That's the author's challenge.... He's talking about a tendency to hold other people in awe, to be controlled and mastered by them, to depend on them for what God alone can give.... [Welch] proposes an antidote: the fear of God ... the believer's response to God's power, majesty, and not least his mercy."
—*Dallas Morning News*

"Refreshingly biblical ... brimming with helpful, readable, practical insight."
—**John MacArthur**, Pastor-Teacher of Grace Community Church; Featured Teacher with the Grace to You Media Ministry

This book takes dead aim at the heart of ongoing sin. Drawing from two masterful works by John Owen, Kris Lundgaard offers insight, encouragement, and hope for overcoming the enemy within.

"A solid reminder that apart from the grace of God we are far weaker than we can imagine—but greater is he that is in us than he that is in the world."
 —**Bryan Chapell,** Author of *Holiness by Grace: Delighting in the Joy That Is Our Strength*

"Fresh, contemporary, highly readable. Every Christian who is serious about holiness should read this book."
 —**Jerry Bridges,** Author of *Respectable Sins: Confronting the Sins We Tolerate*